Learning to Make a Difference

The authors will donate all royalties due to them from sales of this book to the CUPP 'On Our Doorsteps' fund, which supports partnership projects between academics, students and community groups in neighbourhoods close to each of the university campuses.

Learning to Make a Difference

Student–community engagement and
the higher education curriculum

Juliet Millican and Tom Bourner

Published by the National Institute of Adult Continuing Education

(England and Wales)
21 De Montfort Street
Leicester LE1 7GE

Company registration no. 2603322
Charity registration no. 1002775

NIACE is the National Institute of Adult Continuing Education, the national
voice for lifelong learning. We are an internationally respected development
organisation and think-tank, working on issues central to the economic
renewal of the UK, particularly in the political economy, education and
learning, public policy and regeneration fields.

www.niace.org.uk

For details of all our publications, visit http://shop.niace.org.uk

Follow NIACE on Twitter: @NIACEhq
@NIACECymru (Wales)
@NIACEbooks (Publications)

Cataloguing in Publications Data
A CIP record for this title is available from the British Library

978-1-86201-866-2 (Print)
978-1-86201-867-9 (PDF)
978-1-86201-868-6 (ePub)
978-1-86201-869-3 (Kindle)

All websites referenced in this book were correct and accessible at the time of
going to press.

The views expressed in this publication are not necessarily endorsed by the
publisher.

Cover design by Patrick Armstrong Book Production Services
Designed and typeset by Avon DataSet Ltd, Bidford on Avon, Warwickshire.
Printed in the UK by Marston Book Services, Abingdon

Contents

Section Three: Reflecting on Student–Community Engagement

Introduction

Student–community engagement

Student–community engagement (SCE) refers to students being involved in community projects local to their university. It normally involves the inclusion within the higher education (HE) curriculum of a period of time during which students work for a community-based organisation in ways that enable them to benefit the community and to learn from the experience. It is the term which was adopted in 2008 by CUPP, the Community University Partnership Programme at the University of Brighton, to cover accredited, engaged work that makes a contribution to not-for-profit organisations within its locality, while also forming a valuable part of students' learning. The term is also used more widely within the UK to refer to engaged and experiential learning that is mutually beneficial and is part of a broader field of community–university engagement.

SCE can take many forms, ranging from accredited volunteering, where there are attempts to distil learning from students' volunteering experiences, to the sort of fully-blown 'service learning' commonly found in US universities, and from community-based research in Canada to transformational programmes of higher education in Africa. It can be a core part of the HE curriculum or it can be a single option within a modular programme, and can provide valuable hands on experience particularly for academic subjects that would not otherwise involve a practice experience. Other terms for this work have included 'pedagogies for civic engagement', 'education for active citizenship' and 'engaged learning'. A strong feature of student–community engagement is reciprocity, i.e. the 'give and take' involved,

1

as students invest time and energy in community-based activity and gain valuable experience in working with people, developing projects and applying new skills in real contexts. The implication is that real-world learning, which exposes students to new experiences and diverse groups, contributes to students becoming more mature, able and aware graduates who are more likely to continue to take an active role in their communities.

SCE fits within the 'third leg' or third stream of a university's mission, often understood to be teaching, research and service or external engagement with organisations or groups outside of its immediate community of students and university employees. This third stream is increasingly becoming recognised as a priority alongside its other two concerns of teaching and research.

While universities have always had a societal element and a moral dimension, these have come to the fore at different times in their history and this book traces that history from the earliest universities to the present day. For the past 20 years, engagement outside of the institution, involvement with industry and the need to prove the impact of research and to facilitate public access to science have come to the fore again in the UK, and community–university engagement forms a core part of this work. During the same period there has been a growing recognition of the importance of developing students' capacity for, and disposition towards, social responsibility and active citizenship.

The legitimacy behind a university's involvement in the social responsibility of its students can be found in the danger of focusing on the pursuit of knowledge without placing this knowledge in a broader social context. It was such an environment in which the amoral pursuit of science could flourish in the early decades of the twentieth century and, with hindsight, this contributed to the role played by the universities in the rise of fascism in Germany and caused many people to question this view of the purpose of a university education. By the end of the twentieth century there were probably few people who would challenge the proposition that there is a moral dimension to education at all levels, including HE. This leaves open the question of *how* to address this issue within universities and other HE institutions.★ Possibilities have included discussion of values within the curriculum,

---

★ The moral dimension of a higher education is more easily addressed in some university subjects (such as health studies and social sciences including education) than others (such as maths, modern languages or chemistry).

critical engagement with the application of theoretical ideas and the link between education, experience and service.

The scope of this book

Developing students' understanding of questions of equality and social justice, and a sense of social responsibility, is an outcome central to student–community engagement programmes and this book has been written as a response to this. The first section looks at the history of the university and the place of engagement or social responsibility within it. It traces the different priorities given to teaching, research and third-stream work and the changing view of moral or social involvement. It also looks at direct influences on SCE and other forms of engaged learning that have sprung up in different parts of the world. It makes a pedagogic case for experiential learning and looks in some depth at the different forms of learning that might emerge from this. It uses terms like social concern, civic responsibility and community participation to justify the inclusion of SCE in mainstream, discipline-based study. It argues that HE is not only subject-centred but is also society-centred and that SCE adds a dimension to university education which may otherwise be limited to the pursuit of knowledge and understanding of an academic subject.

Section Two sets out to provide some practical support in designing and developing SCE within a university setting, showing how learning from community engagement can enrich a university education. It addresses the question of how to position SCE within the curriculum, how to design modules, the kinds of projects students might work on and the institutional and pedagogical issues that might arise when planning learning in partnership with community organisations. It offers some practical examples of module outlines and learning agreements and guidance on how to connect and work with local groups

Section Three provides some case studies written by students or community partners associated with CUPP, which outline the benefits and the pitfalls of this work. It offers in-depth reflections on what each has gained from working with the other and tries to draw out lessons for other organisations just embarking on this work.

While there has been considerable activity in this area for some time, particularly in the context of North America, there have been many recent developments in other parts of the world, including the

UK. However, so far relatively little has been written about SCE in the context of UK HE and this book aims to redress that balance. It is based on the experience and knowledge gained by the SCE work of CUPP at the University of Brighton over the past ten years which has had some influence on the development of SCE both nationally and internationally throughout that period.

This book, by drawing on the work of CUPP, tends to use the term 'community engagement' to refer to CUPP's involvement with local individuals, organisations and groups in ways that are mutually beneficial. CUPP prioritises those partnerships that tackle disadvantage or promote sustainable development through building capacity at community level, promoting student involvement in the local community or carrying out applied research in response to community requests. Other universities use terms such as 'social engagement' (to focus more on activities designed to develop social capital within the local environment), or 'public engagement', which prioritises the involvement of specialists with non-specialists, or public involvement in science (HEFCE, 2006). While these terms are sometimes used concomitantly, they also have important differences.

Readership

This book is aimed at everyone interested in new developments in UK HE. It will obviously be of particular interest to people involved in developing university–community engagement and especially:

- academics engaged in curriculum design and development;
- those involved in various forms of SCE, including service learning and student volunteering;
- senior staff who increasingly recognise the importance of university–community developments;
- staff working in staff development sections of universities; and
- people working in related fields such as careers advisers who will recognise SCE as a way of developing student employability.

The examples and case studies may, furthermore, be pertinent to people working in other areas of education and broader employment fields who are keen to develop their capacity to engage with their local communities. The issues raised and the experiences of participants and community groups would not be dissimilar to those associated with schools developing links for citizenship programmes or employers working on corporate responsibility initiatives.

This book is based on the recognition of the equal value of different forms of knowledge and the importance of being able to bring together the knowledge drawn from personal experience, from practitioner or professional work and from academic study. SCE sets out to introduce students to the way in which diverse knowledge can work together for a more holistic understanding of a particular situation or context. It draws from the work of Gibbons *et al.* (1994) on Mode 1 and Mode 2 knowledge. Mode 1 knowledge is 'pure, disciplinary, homogenous, expert-led, supply driven, peer reviewed and almost exclusively university based' (Hart *et al.*, 2007) while Mode 2 knowledge is applied, problem centred, trans-disciplinary... and increasingly handled outside higher education institutions' (Hart *et al.*, 2007, p. 5).

This book is particularly directed towards those working in universities and other institutions and involved in the design, development, management and delivery of courses or modules involving student learning from community engagement. It includes critical assessments of important developments in the emerging field of SCE with particular attention to student *learning* from community engagement. This reflects the backgrounds of the authors, one of whom has worked as development manager for the SCE strand of CUPP at the University of Brighton and is currently its deputy director, and the other of whom is a professor of personal and professional development.

Current student engagement programmes can often be loosely grouped under two broad banners – those that offer practical, experiential opportunities for student involvement, which are referred to in the USA as 'service learning', and those that involve students in research partnerships, sometimes known as 'science shops'. Service learning, as its name suggests, links a service experience with a civil society organisation with specific curricula outcomes. It emerged from a period in US history when a new generation of faculty, recruited in response to growing numbers of students, brought to the universities values, concerns and interests that had been moulded by the civil rights movement and the protest movements of the early 1970s (Stanton, Giles and Cruz, 1999). Frustrated by the narrowness of disciplinary research the faculties wanted to apply their scholarship to the pressing issues of the day and link these into the courses they offered their students (Peterman, 2005). A service learning experience requires students to take on a period of activity within their locality not dissimilar to volunteering. But the curricula requirements of critical reflection, policy analysis, working with diverse groups and understanding inequality first hand move the experience beyond the offer of practical help to a deeper level of understanding. The requirements usually include some reference to a local and a global community and involve strong links to civil society groups, opportunities for students to work in partnership, critical reflection on process and personal values and development, and the need to bring together the competing agendas of policy, theory and practice. They encourage students to take a broader view of what constitutes knowledge and to work with both academic and theoretical knowledge frameworks and the experiential knowledge of practitioners.

Science shops came out of a particular period in Dutch universities when students had fully-funded degree programmes that were not time bound. They became access points to which local community members or pressure groups could bring research issues that students would take up on their behalf. By bringing together the energy and initiative of a student with the experience of a community group and the expertise of an academic supervisor, they have been able to add scientific evidence to significant local issues. They have expanded from the hard sciences to include the humanities and soft sciences and are able to provide valuable research information for community groups, while offering a significant learning opportunity in interpersonal skills, local politics and applied research (Farakas, 2002).

The history of both of these initiatives are explored in more depth in Chapter Two of this book but the current context is very different from that of the 1970s when students had more time to study, were often more politically motivated and were less concerned with questions of student debt and future employment. The term 'service' is also less transferable outside of the USA, where it tends to carry overtones of welfare, rather than a rights-based or advocacy approach to development. While many current programmes are more concerned with equality and the development of citizenship, citizenship education has, at least in the UK, assumed a rather negative profile as a result of compulsory secondary school programmes. Despite the social responsibility of a university having assumed a strong strategic profile, community engagement may on the surface not seem an easy fit with a twenty-first century university paid for largely through undergraduate fees (Millican, 2014).

Dominant trends in the current context

While the different forms of SCE emerge from a range of different histories, they share the aim of developing more rounded and compe-tent professionals and value both academic and practitioner knowledge. Although such programmes are not new, they are becoming more significant internationally, particularly in relation to questions of citizenship, employability and social justice. At the time of publication and well into the second decade of the twenty-first century, the role of HE worldwide and the context in which it operates is clearly shifting. The model of universities that dominated during most of the twentieth century no longer seems to fit a world where universities are seen as more accountable to the societies in which they are located and where there has been a revolution in HE participation rates.

There has been a huge increase in demand for HE over the past 50 years, with enrolments worldwide increasing six times (from 13 million to 82 million) between 1960 and 1995, and almost doubling again in a single decade to 143 million in 2006. The number of female enrolments has risen from well under, to well over, half of all students in the past ten years. This is against a global population rise in the same period from 3 billion in 1960 to 6.5 billion in 2006 (*Global World Report on Higher Education*). As a result, states are unable to fund HE provision, and many countries have seen the development of private sector institutions and increased fees within state-led provision. Debates about whether or not HE should be considered a private good (helping the most able individuals to build glittering careers to gain personal advantage) or a public good (adding value to society by educating productive citizens capable of addressing the world's key problems on both a local and a global scale) have emerged in the consideration of whether HE should be funded by individuals, employers or the state. The move towards personal finance of HE has contributed to the view of HE as an investment, with students anticipating a return on their investment in terms of future earnings. When students are situated as clients and customers, there is a danger that they will act more as passive consumers than active learners. This detracts from their ability to learn and develop personally and inhibits their future potential to be active citizens.

The 1998 World Conference on Higher Education in Paris was convened by UNESCO to re-examine educational policies in the context of the new millennium. It included representatives from 182 countries and its 15 fundamental principles included equality of access, the use of knowledge generated for the benefit of society, the importance of reflection on the ethical dimensions of knowledge and a concern with strengthening the identities and values of students. The declaration it produced emphasised the value of education in socio-cultural and economic development and the importance of social responsibility. HE institutions were seen as having a key role in creating 'citizens of the world', capable of committing themselves to addressing global problems, valuing diversity and promoting a culture of peace. A 'third stream' of social and economic engagement was recognised alongside HE's goals of teaching and research, as was the need to ensure that teaching, research and dissemination were 'mutually enriching' with tangible outcomes for society. The declaration also included the need for accreditation and rigorous quality assurance procedures linked to regional frameworks that would enable students to move between institutions in neighbouring countries.

The past decade and a half has seen the impact of this, with an increased awareness of the social responsibility of universities and the emergence of mechanisms which link higher-level study and research to current issues of local, national and global concern. Third-stream work with both employers and community groups is becoming as much a part of the mission of many universities around the world as teaching and research. A number of international networks have been established, committed to sharing experiences and supporting institutions in implementing the priorities of the UNESCO declaration. The Talloires Network, set up in 2005 by Tufts University in the USA, is an international association of institutions committed to strengthening the civic roles and social responsibilities of HE, with members in Europe, Africa, Asia, the Pacific, the Americas and the Caribbean. The University Social Responsibility Alliance, established in California in 2009, is concerned with promoting societal responsibility in teaching in the USA and beyond, and has hosted a number of conferences across South-East Asia. The Global University Network for Innovation was created in Barcelona in 1999 by UNESCO to facilitate the main decisions coming out of the 1998 World Conference on Higher Education and has a strong network of members. Between them, they are working

> *What has become clear is that none of these major issues in the global agenda will be resolved without the participation of universities, since they are the environments that foster not only knowledge thought and research but also proposals for social action.* (Ramon de la Fuente, President of the International Association of Universities, 2010)

In addition, boundaries between sectors are shifting and blurring. As governments become less able to fund and manage public services, these are being franchised to voluntary and third-sector organisations. Civil society organisations have been forced to tender for funds on a competitive basis and adopt some of the strategies of short-term contracts more familiar to private sector organisations, while private sector bodies are drawn in to service provision through sponsorship and corporate social responsibility. Individuals are no longer assured of a job in one organisation or even one sector for life. Future professionals will need to be able to operate in partnership with those from very different backgrounds and policy areas and organisations will need to be receptive to new structures and demands.

For universities to thrive within this climate, they need to work in partnership with regional and national decision-makers as well as international pressure groups and local communities. Rather than see-ing themselves solely in terms of the production and dissemination of knowledge, they need to better understand how knowledge is built, and the value of – and connections between – different forms of knowledge, and between knowledge, understanding and action. Consequently, they also need to become skilled in knowledge brokering and knowledge exchange. This may mean a review of their vision and mission, a shift in institutional structures within and between disciplines and new approaches to the ways in which knowledge is generated and transmitted. Community–university partnership activity, action research programmes and the use of community-, and participative research approaches all provide mechanisms which bring together academic and practitioner-based knowledge on common problems. Their students will need a personal appreciation of difference and first-hand knowledge of how to deal with diversity. They will need to be able to apply learned knowledge, to work within and outside of organisational structures and with others from different sectors and discipline backgrounds. They will need an understanding of national policy initiatives and a sense of their responsibility as global, as well as national, citizens. All of these things need to be reflected in the curricula offered and the pedagogies used to impart it. Such a curricula needs to find space for learners to explore their own values and to test out their aspirations for achievement and change. It needs to provide them with the opportunity to critique and reflect on the knowledge they have gained and compare this with other forms of knowledge and other types of expertise. This suggests that during the next decade, HE professionals will need to find innovative ways to do more with less. Chapters Three and Four of this book explore this changing context in more depth and make a strong case for how SCE might respond to the pressures now facing universities in many parts of the world.

In the twenty-first century the problems facing humanity, on both a local and a global scale, include how to deal with climate change, the conflict that arises from the marginalisation of minorities, and competition for limited resources. In essence how human beings might best live with each other within the environments they share. Although the claims made for community engagement may be many and varied it is important to avoid the rhetoric and begin to examine, practically, ways in which students, as professionals of the next generation, are introduced to some of these problems within their local community and involved in developing strategies to address them. Inevitably these will be strategies that cross discipline boundaries, that include community and practitioner as well as university knowledge and that require a broad range of approaches. By drawing on examples from a specific UK context, this book attempts to illustrate some of these approaches which in the end are facing HE institutions in many parts of the world.

References

Bourner, T. (2004) 'The broadening of the higher education curriculum, 1970–2002', *Higher Education Review*, 36(2), pp. 45–58.

Bourner, T. (2008) 'The fully-functioning university', *Higher Education Review*, 40(2), pp. 26–45.

De la Fuente, R. (2010) *Higher Education and Social Construction*, Interview for the GUNI newsletter, May 2010.

Farakas, N.E. (2002) *Bread, Cheese and Expertise, Dutch Science Shops and Democratic Institutions*. Available at: www.livingknowledge.org/livingknowledge/wp.../02/Farkas-thesis.pdf

Gibbons, M., Limoges, C., Nowotny, H., Shwartzman, S., Scott, P. and Trow,

M. (1994) *The New Production of Knowledge.* London: Sage.

GUNI (2009) *Higher Education at a Time of Transformation, New Dynamics for Social Responsibility.* Synthesis of the GUNI Higher Education in the World Reports, GUNI, Barcelona.

Humboldt, W. von (1970) 'On the Spirit and Organisational Framework of Intellectual Institutions in Berlin', *Minerva*, 8, pp 242–67 (German original 1810).

Hart, A., Maddison, E. and Wolff, D. (2007) *Community University Partnerships in Practice.* Leicester: NIACE.

Millican, J. (2007) *Community University Engagement: A Model for the 21st Century?* Paper presented at Global Citizens Conference, University of Bournemouth, September 2007.

Millican, J. (2014) 'Engagement and employability: Student expectations of higher education', *AISHE-J: The All Ireland Journal of Teaching and Learning in Higher Education*, 6(1).

Peterman, W. (2005) *Community Engagement and the Research University: Unrealistic Expectations or New Opportunities?* Benjamin Meaker Lecture, University of Bristol.

Stanton, T., Giles, D. and Cruz, N. (1999) *Service-Learning.* San Francisco: Jossey-Bass.

Taylor, P (2008) *Higher Education in the World: New Challenges and Emerging Roles for Human and Social Development, Introduction to GUNI world report.* Palgrave Macmillan.

UNESCO (2009) 'The New Dynamics of Higher Education and Research For Societal Change and Development;. COMMUNIQUE 8 July 2009. Paris: UNESCO.

Section One

Understanding Student–Community Engagement

In the beginning: The origins and history of the university and its three missions

Introduction

This chapter is about the historical roots of a university and the deep context of SCE. It looks at what it means to be a university and where SCE fits in to the range of activities a university has undertaken at different periods in its history. In doing so, it justifies SCE and the broader world of community engagement as a long-term, legitimate part of a university. The chapter explores the changing relationship between SCE and the three goals or missions of the university, illustrating how the political and social context have brought different goals to the fore at different times. Understanding how a university's third mission has responded to social and political pressures in the past sets the scene for current engagement initiatives.

The three distinct stages of the development of the university

In order to explore the history and development of SCE within universities, it helps to be clear about what it means to be an institution of HE and the history and development of the university itself. The Western university has passed through three broad and distinct stages:

- The medieval university, which lasted until about the end of the fifteenth century
- The Renaissance and early modern university, which was

triggered by its disengagement from the Latin Church and
lasted until the nineteenth century

- The Humboldtian university, which has its origins in
  the development of the knowledge-led institutions in
  Germany in the nineteenth century

In the first stage, the Western university of the Middle Ages started as an
institution of the Latin Church, no less than a cathedral or a monastery.
It was run by clerics, with instruction given by them and tuition in
Latin, the mother tongue of the Latin Church. It was subject to canon
(ecclesiastical) law rather than civil law and it was exempt from fiscal
exactions of civic or national authorities. The papacy licensed universities
so that their degrees were recognised throughout Latin Christendom,
wherever papal writ ran. Successful graduates were awarded the *licentia
docendi*, the license to teach in any university. In this stage the university
existed primarily to serve Western Christendom by preparing students
for the priesthood and by advancing knowledge through dissemination
and interpretation of spiritual knowledge and the accumulation of
knowledge from other civilisations, particularly from Islamic countries
and from ancient Greece (Bourner, 2008).

In the second stage, around the time of the Renaissance, the university
became independent of the Latin Church and its focus shifted from the
needs of that Church to the needs of the members of the university
itself, i.e. the fellows and the students. Income from endowments and
the fees of students from well-heeled and well-connected families meant
that the post-medieval universities had sufficient financial autonomy to
give them considerable discretion to follow their own destinies. In this
stage, the university curriculum became less Church-focused and more
student-focused. It opened up the domains of recognised knowledge to
a range of new academic subjects and new fields of enquiry. The range
of university subjects expanded and university education became more
humanitarian, classical and liberal. The university acquired freedom to
offer a higher education fit for a 'godly gentleman' and for leadership in
a variety of different fields in the young nation state. The university of
the Renaissance and early modern period was a civilising force in times
that were still in many ways wild, philistine and brutish.

The third stage is characterised by increased emphasis on the
advancement of knowledge, by the admission of empirical knowledge
into the university and by subject specialisation. The university in this

stage is sometimes known as the Humboldtian university in recognition of role played by William von Humboldt in conceiving it and then acting as midwife to its birth in early-nineteenth-century Prussia. The Humboldtian university sought the advancement of knowledge through the pursuit of new knowledge. In this stage a subject-focused education replaced the student-focused education of the earlier period by developing the critical faculties of scholars and opening the doors to empirical knowledge. It also sought to benefit those outside the institution by enhancing material well-being through greater understanding and control of the material world. The heyday of the Humboldtian university was the high years of the twentieth century but, as explored below, it was increasingly challenged in the later decades.

This brief summary of the main endeavours of the academy in each of its developmental stages has a number of implications for what it means to be a university in the twenty-first century. Firstly, in every stage of its development, the university has had the same three basic concerns:

1. To provide for the higher education of students
2. To contribute to the advancement of knowledge
3. To benefit those beyond the walls of the university

Table 1.1 (over) summarises the main focus of each of these concerns in the three stages of the development of the university.

It is reasonable to conclude that to warrant the name 'university' it is necessary that an institution endeavours to contribute to the advancement of knowledge and the higher education of students and be of benefit to those outside the institution. It seems as if historically the two principle roles of a university, i.e. teaching and research, have always been seen in different ways in relation to the needs of society. In each of the three eras of the university's history there has been a key driver, or funder – the Church, the Enlightenment and then industry – that has had a say in how these two roles related to broader societal needs and ultimately influenced what was taught and what was researched. How that meeting of societal needs happened and the mechanisms for relating outside the academy became over time seen as a third important function, or – as it is technically called – part of the *tripartite* mission. This raises the question as to whether we are in fact entering a fourth era, when rising unemployment, climate change and the problems associated

Table 1.1. Main focus of endeavours in each of the mains stages of the Western university

	Relationship to those outside the university campus	The higher education of students	The advancement of knowledge
Stage 1: The medieval university	Service to the Latin Church with its aim to save the immortal souls of Western Christendom.	Preparing students for a vocation in the Latin Church	Accumulating and interpreting such knowledge from Islam and Classical Antiquity as could be reconciled with Christian scripture.
Stage 2: The early modern university	Contributing to the civilisation of those who would hold high office in the learned professions and the young nation state.	Developing godly gentlemen who could tell right from wrong morally, intellectually, socially and aesthetically.	Enlarging the domain of academic knowledge by opening up new fields of enquiry beyond that prescribed by the Latin Church.
Stage 3: The Humboldtian university	Contributing to greater understanding and control of the world in which we live and increasing the material well-being of people.	Developing critical faculties of students and their ability to apply them to up-to-date knowledge of a recognised academic subject.	Enlarging the stock of academic knowledge through research and the recognition of empirical knowledge.

Note: A full account of the derivation of this table can be found in Bourner (2008).

with globalisation when servicing industry are being called into question. This opens the space for other forms of external engagement that are more concerned with social agendas, sustainable development and community needs.

A second conclusion is that in each of these stages, one part of the tripartite mission has dominated the other two. In the medieval university the dominant goal was service to the Latin Church and through it the people of Western Christendom. In the early modern period the dominant goal was to provide a higher education for students, drawn mostly from well-heeled and well-connected families whose fees made a significant contribution to funding the colleges. And in the Humboldtian university the dominant goal was the advancement of knowledge in recognised subjects of study.

A third conclusion is that as one of the three areas has become dominant, the other two parts have been interpreted and expressed in ways that have served the dominant part. In the medieval university, service dominated as the medieval university directly served the Latin Church and its main concern was saving the souls of Western Christendom. It therefore provided a higher education that equipped students to serve the Church and the people of Western Christendom through the priesthood. The particular forms that the advancement of knowledge then took were dissemination of the Word of God, interpretation of Holy Writ (i.e. scholarship) and the accumulation of such secular knowledge as could be reconciled with Christian scripture.

In the second great epoch of university development, the Renaissance and early modern period, the universities were financially independent of the Latin Church, depending on the fruits of earlier endowments and the fees of students. The dominant purpose of the university was the higher education of those students and universities contributed to the advancement of knowledge by legitimising new fields of academic study. It was the age when the humanities gained entry to the university. Without the requirement to study subjects that supported service to the Church, there was increasing interest in the classics and scope for fellows to indulge their own interests in the pursuit of knowledge. The highest goal of HE was to develop 'godly gentlemen', leaders for the new nation state and the learned professions, who were a civilising influence in what was still a barbaric age.

The third stage, the Humboldtian university, was when the advancement of knowledge became the dominant part of the mission and the nature of a university education changed again to serve that dominant goal. The 'service' part of the university mission was interpreted in ways that reflected the new dominance with an emphasis on the enlargement of the pool of knowledge from which everyone drew, increasing mastery of the physical world and the development of critical faculties to expose those who would seek to mislead through error or deception.

'Traditional university education' and the advancement of knowledge

It was in this third stage of development, the Humboldtian or 'modern' university of the nineteenth and twentieth centuries, that HE changed to serve the advancement of knowledge as the dominant goal. The early modern university that preceded it had relatively little subject specialisation with all students studying basically the same classics curriculum (including, at Cambridge, classical maths) with the aim of producing gentlemen (at a time when all students were male) who would grace any of the learned professions especially the Anglican Church. By contrast, a university education that serves the advancement of knowledge was deemed to include the most up-to-date knowledge and the development of critical faculties to test ideas and evidence within the context of a subject discipline. Hague (1991) summarised this position saying, 'Academics must believe that acquiring the ability to test ideas and evidence is the primary benefit of a university education' (Hague, 1991, p. 64).

It was widely believed that understanding of a subject could be achieved by the application of critical thinking to subject knowledge. The equation was straightforward: Knowledge (K) plus Critical thinking (C) equals Understanding (U): $K + C = U$, and it was believed that this would ensure the employability of graduates. The development of the ability to test ideas and evidence was seen as the core process of higher education and the key to both subject understanding and graduate employability. For university lecturers, this had the great merit that they could concentrate on the acquisition of subject understanding through the development of critical thinking and consequently did not need to concern themselves additionally with graduate employability per se.

The task of a lecturer was relatively straightforward: keep up to date with the new knowledge in the subject through the process of scholarship and disseminate it in a way that encouraged the development of the students' critical faculties. Lectures, books and journals were the main vehicle for realising the former; and practicals and seminars (a teaching method imported into English universities from German universities in the early decades of the twentieth century) were the main ways of realising the latter. The advancement of knowledge demanded increasing specialisation, with the result that the number of academic subjects in which a degree could be obtained steadily multiplied.

The task seemed a timeless one; the teachers of the 1970s had experienced it as students in the 1960s, 1950s or the 1940s. Those who became lecturers in HE institutions had, presumably, a relatively successful experience as students. Their academic qualifications certified that they had gained up-to-date knowledge, developed the ability to test ideas and evidence and acquired a good understanding of an academic discipline. As teachers they could model the process that had been successfully applied to them to produce the next generation of graduates with up-to-date knowledge and well-honed critical faculties.

In the 1970s it was difficult to find any courses in academic practice to prepare lecturers for teaching in HE, as it was assumed they would adopt the teaching methods they had themselves experienced as students. Their well-honed critical faculties should, in theory, ensure a high and rising level of academic excellence over time.

In that sense, this curriculum had a 'steady-state' quality about it and can reasonably be termed the 'traditional' model of HE. Such a traditional model could be critiqued on the basis that it was:

- *an excessively narrow form of education and lacked breadth, that students were learning more and more about less and less.;*
- *it lacked any of the former moral strand within higher education and had become a purely technical;*
- *it prepared students to contribute to the advancement of knowledge as researchers or teachers but not for any other kind of professional employment.*

(Bourner and Rospigliosi, 2008b)

The emphasis on research and scholarship gave rise to the charge that institutions were becoming 'ivory towers' divorced from the concerns of the rest of society and these criticisms led to the establishment of polytechnics to give more emphasis to those who would follow a range of professional employments that served local and regional communities

(Watson, 2007). This had the paradoxical result of taking pressure off the universities who could point to the polytechnics as the institutions where that sort of HE was located.

The broadening of the HE curriculum after 1980

Graduate unemployment in the 1980s and its effect on the consensus on the traditional curriculum

Most defenders of the 'traditional' model of university education that pertained during the middle half of the twentieth century believed that the employment of graduates was assured by their capacity to test ideas and think critically – and this was seen as the hallmark of graduate-level jobs. At that time, relatively few school leavers went on to HE so the majority of students were the most capable learners and their employment prospects were already relatively good.

However, during the early 1980s there was a rapid rise in unemployment among new graduates. Records showing the destinations of graduates at the end of their graduating year, showed sudden high unemployment and evidence that graduates were taking jobs which, in earlier decades, would not have been viewed as 'graduate level' and which made relatively few demands on their finely honed critical faculties (Tarsh, 1982). More and more lecturers became concerned that they had placed too much trust in 'the ability to test ideas and evidence' as the core learning outcome of HE. Widespread concern about graduate unemployment resulted in increasing scepticism about the 'traditional' curriculum model and opened the door to the 'transferable skills' movement.

As the unemployment of new graduates rose, more lecturers were prepared to find room in the curriculum for the development of skills beyond the capacity to test ideas and evidence. There had never been a shortage of people advocating more vocational relevance in the HE curriculum, particularly in the colleges that became the polytechnics (for example Robinson, 1968), but while university students had been able to find employment after graduation, their influence was limited. As graduate unemployment rose, lecturers started to pay more attention to those advocating curriculum reform directed at tackling this.

Efforts were directed at identifying what employers wanted students to be able to *do* upon graduation and long lists of transferable skills that would contribute to 'work-readiness' were compiled. Research was commissioned to identify the skills needed for successful graduate employment, which led to reports such as *Skills for Graduates in the 21st Century* (AGR, 1995). Some of these skills seemed remarkably low, suggesting that HE was lowering its sights from the pursuit of 'excellence' to the pursuit of 'competence' and potentially demonstrating a 'dumbing-down' of HE. Lecturers were divided between those advocating 'transferable skills' and those who felt 'the development of critical faculties' had not gone far enough. Barnett (1994, 1997) argued for the extension of the HE curriculum to cover the application of critical thinking from a narrow concern with subject disciplines to the student as a person and to the student's action in the world.

Faced with the 'reality' of rising graduate unemployment there was no shortage of explanations for the breakdown of the traditional model. Researchers at the Institute of Manpower Studies★ (for example Pearson and Baker, 1984) offered evidence that only about one-third of graduates entered employment in which their subject knowledge was used. This meant that, as far as the HE curriculum was concerned, the employability of the remaining two-thirds of graduates depended solely on the development of their critical faculties. Rising graduate unemployment indicated that employers wanted more than the 'the ability to test ideas and evidence'. The Royal Society for Arts argued that what employers (and the economy) wanted was people who could innovate and develop, whereas the educational curriculum at all levels (and especially in HE) developed people who could only critically evaluate. It led a campaign, 'Education for Capability', aimed at broadening and refocusing the educational curriculum on creating rather than critiquing. By the end of the 1980s the belief in the adequacy of subject knowledge and well-honed critical faculties had been undermined, making possible a range of curriculum innovations of which transferable skills became the most influential.

In the early 1990s, the number of transferable skills that contribute to graduate employability seemed to rise rapidly and with it a concern that 'developing critical faculties' might be lost among newly identified competencies (see, for example, Barnett, 1994). This led to a debate about graduate standards and the nature of 'graduateness' (for example HEQC, 1997a, b). As the UK moved from an elite system of HE to a

---

★ Now the Institute of Employment Studies.

mass system of HE in the early 1990s, lecturers were more exercised by trying to resolve the increasing pressures from a rising numbers of students. Many university teachers experienced increasing stress as the under-funded expansion of HE caused the ratio of students to staff to rise. These day-to-day difficulties exerted a much more powerful force on the nature of the HE curriculum than either the 'competencies' or the 'graduateness' debates.

Inevitably this led to less face-to-face contact, with students taking more responsibility for their own learning and a shift in the curriculum. Students would receive less content input from lecturers and more process support for autonomous learning. This included the encouragement of student independence and a shift in the role of lecturer from disseminating information and leading small-group discussion towards more indirect ways of supporting learning. It became clear that this approach was embedded in a philosophy less prosaic than simply coping with more students and extended to the curriculum itself, i.e. it was not simply about *how* to teach but also about *what* to teach, a philosophy that was adopted by the advocates of 'lifelong learning':

> ... *our ultimate goal in higher education must be to encourage students to be responsible for, and in control of their own learning...*
> (Zuber-Skerrett, 1992, p. 24)

In addition, the early 1990s saw a growing awareness of the accelerating pace of change in the economy. Graduate jobs had traditionally offered the prospect of professional careers or at least greater employment stability, but this was becoming rarer at a time when the number of candidates for graduate jobs was rising.

In much the same way that the Humboldtian vision of a university had elevated 'critical thinking' from a means to an end, so lifelong learning elevated the 'ability to plan and manage own learning' from a means to an end; what started as a way of coping with larger numbers of students ended in a new curriculum for HE. At a superficial level, this meant that the universities must prepare themselves for people to enter universities at different times of their lives. This led to the development of courses for postgraduates to 'top up' with the latest knowledge at regular intervals throughout their lives and to an undergraduate body that would no longer be dominated by school leavers. It suggested a wider range of postgraduate provision, ranging from short courses to professional doctorates aimed at the leading edge of professional practice.

Ultimately, the goal of lifelong learning meant 'the development of students' capacities to plan and manage their own learning'. From this perspective, *what* students learn is less important than *how* they learn. Learning how to learn became a learning outcome in its own right; the process became the product.

Increasingly, the paraphernalia associated with autonomous learning started to enter universities: learning contracts, learning logs, portfolios of evidence and so on. This was new territory for university lecturers and universities increasingly offered courses on teaching with this new focus. At many universities, participation in these courses became a condition of employment for new lecturers. A study of these courses (Bourner *et al.*, 2003) found that for the most part they were not preparing lecturers to give more professional and effective lectures, seminars and tutorials, but expanding the repertoire of lecturers in ways that they would help them to support students in becoming autonomous learners.

The underfunded expansion of student numbers in the early 1990s also had an impact in two other main ways:

1. Unemployment of new graduates rose again. This ensured that transferable skills for work readiness did not slip off the agenda.
2. The enlarged student body was more heterogeneous than earlier generations of students. This supported the movement towards more autonomous learning which offered a way of catering for the more diverse range of learning needs.

Concern with graduate unemployment had focused attention on skills for employment and the accelerating pace of change in the economy, which meant any set of graduate skills would become outdated before long (Knight, 1998). The emergent question was, 'How could universities best enhance the prospects of graduates in the context of accelerating technological, economic and social change?' The most compelling response was to prepare students to become lifelong learners and to plan and manage the achievement of their own learning goals. Another was to be able to capture the learning that is available as a natural by-product of living and particularly working. The term 'reflective learning' was increasingly heard in connection with the term 'lifelong learning'. It seemed that effective lifelong learners needed to plan and manage their own learning outcomes and be able to capture emergent learning. Reflection seemed key to experiential learning and the role of reflection in learning was already established in the works of educators such as Dewey, Schon, Kolb and Boud. It was this broadening of the curriculum to include reflective learning that allowed the entry of SCE into universities. While there is considerable variation in the form SCE takes in different institutions, reflective learning is a core element of the learning process.

Rebalancing the tripartite mission in the twentieth century

Universities were 'elite' institutions during the Humboldtian period when the percentage of the population with a university education was in less than single figures (i.e. less than one per cent). During the 1960s, with less than ten per cent of school leavers going on to university, most stayed in the education system after graduation (Bourner and Rospigliosi, 2008b).★ But by 2000, the first destinations of most new graduates were *outside* the education system and it is harder to justify a form of education that prioritises the pursuit of knowledge in an academic subject when the majority of students leave the academic system, and wider participation has led to a questioning of the Humboldtian goal. New trends emerged, such as work-based learning, community-based learning, problem-based learning, the development of skills for graduate employment, project-based learning and reflective learning.

Over the last century these new trends have in part played a role in moving the university from a peripheral position in the community to a more central feature. Universities are now more dependent on their local communities both for prospective students and to host students through placements and provide the projects that are vital to equipping students with the skills they need for their preferred futures. Concurrently, steps have been taken to break down the 'town and gown' divide that came to the fore in the late 1950s/early 1960s after the intense focus in the early part of the century where it was felt that a key to national economic success was research, particularly scientific, and universities became responsible for a growing share of research in society, elevating the importance attached to the advancement of knowledge.

★ They went on to research, a higher degree (research or taught), teacher training or some other aspect of education

The notion of a 'third stream' is an international concept, used in universities in different parts of the world. Laredo (2007) traces it back to the establishment of research and development activities after World War II. As a notion it connected earlier ideas on the autonomy of universities as a 'republic of scholars' with a new paradigm of 'fundamental research' which is both open and available (Laredo, 2007, p. 2). He traces an emerging role of universities in innovation processes. Such processes require a more collaborative approach with other sectors and the gradual extension of this from working with the private sector to the consideration of collective actors working on civil society issues. Laredo comments on how increasingly expectations of a third mission have become linked with local development issues.

By the end of the twentieth century the three parts of the university mission were more evenly balanced than in the high years of the twentieth century when the Humboldtian ideal dominated. The service part of the tripartite mission has become more important in its own right as government has increased public financial support to universities. Public expenditure on universities rocketed during the second half of the twentieth century, raising expectations of their contribution to the wider community. Universities began to produce mission statements, which make reference to all three of the tripartite areas, which until the 1980s seemed unnecessary since the mission of a university was self-evidently the advancement of knowledge. During the same period, the teaching element of the tripartite mission became more important through widening participation initiatives and increasing numbers entering HE. Finally, the elevation of the polytechnics and some colleges to university status in the 1990s doubled the number of universities, and polytechnics had been created to support professional employment and to serve local/regional communities.

The twenty-first century and the neoliberal university

Towards the end of the twentieth century, the relative affluence of fully funded students living on government grants in the 1970s and 80s and the rise of activism that accompanied this resulted in various initiatives in which students took a lead in addressing local social concerns. These are discussed in more depth in the following chapter but they laid the ground for initiatives such as the world declaration on HE (1999) and the 2009 conferences on the role of HE in addressing global challenges. The service learning movement grew in the USA and started in South

Africa as students began to explore how education might look in the new republic. Pockets of initiatives sprung up throughout Europe and in the UK which sought to link curriculum study or academic research more closely with community initiatives. External funding, often from the USA, was offered to a small number of UK universities to experiment with what an engaged university might look like in the UK context and the University of Brighton was among those that took up the challenge. The Talloires declaration for social commitment in HE brought together vice chancellors from universities across the world in Talloires, France, in 2003, to commit to the civic roles and social responsibilities of HE. The Higher Education Funding Council for England (HEFCE) introduced social engagement as a funding stream in 2006 and provided support to community knowledge exchanges alongside its more normal knowledge transfer projects. In 2008, Beacons for Public Engagement was established as a government programme with the aim of promoting culture change in HE through the establishment of six beacons in universities across the UK that developed good practice in linking academic research with public access to knowledge. Measurement of societal impact was included as a criterion in the UK's second Research Excellence Framework (REF) of the twenty-first century (2013).

However, the twenty-first century brought with it additional challenges in the form of the 2008 banking crisis and subsequent economic downturn. With more students wanting to attend universities and states struggling to find ways to fund this, globally the twenty-first century saw a shift to higher student fees and an almost privatised university environment. The trebling of university fees in the UK from £3000 a year to around £9000 in 2012 is not atypical of other Western countries but with limited public funds going in to support universities, the subsequent public or societal responsibility of a university is called into question. Of necessity, universities seemed to begin to operate as markets competing for student numbers and finding ways to hold onto them in order to ensure an income stream. Since the 1990s academics had been discussing the effect of using business models on HE provision (Williams, 1997). Boden and Epstein (2006) suggested that in the early twenty-first century, the student experience was already becoming consumerised.

This was added to by an ongoing concern with graduate employability, emphasised by the global economic crash of 2008. If graduates were unable to secure work for themselves they would be unable to repay their fees and the discourse of employability took over from that of 'transferable skills'. An article by Boden and Nedeva in 2010 suggested these were adversely affecting the curriculum by emphasising a narrow instrumental view of education and learning:

> *We argue that the deployment of the new discourses of employability may perpetuate or even increase the stratification of universities and the education they provide along class lines; and third, contemporary hegemonic employability discourses emphasise the development or 'banking' of narrower and specifically job related skills in preference to capacity-building education and the acquisition of social and cultural capital [Freire 1972.]* (Boden and Nedeva, 2010, p. 38)

They quote UK Government policy that claimed introducing 'fairly substantial fees for students' (p. 40) from 2006 to pay for the massification of HE in England would 'increase social justice' (p. 40) and argue that instead such an approach turns the university into a market place and pushes social justice off the agenda:

> *Terms such as 'global knowledge industry' and 'global knowledge businesses' are increasingly used in policy documents, scholarly writing and journalistic commentary with reference to institutions of higher education. Whereas critics use these terms as pejoratives, advocates use them to encourage universities and colleges to adopt policies and practices that are commensurate with their role as businesses within emerging national and global knowledge industries.* (Boden and Nedeva, 2010)

David Willets, Minister for Universities and Science in 2010, also saw the main benefits of a university education in relation to the individual and that the responsibility of paying for this should also lie with those who would directly benefit:

> *It is not just an economic premium … Graduates are – on average – more healthy, more active in the community and more likely to be engaged in the education of their children. The graduate premium evidence further suggests that it is not unreasonable to expect graduates to make more of a contribution themselves.* (Willetts, 2010)

31

While Mahoney, in his foreword to a report on quality in HE (Gibbs, 2010), saw the benefits as continuing to be collective, civic and social:

> *Higher education should be a transformative process that supports the development of graduates who can make a meaningful contribution to wider society, local communities and to the economy.* (Gibbs, 2010, p. 2)

There continues to be a real tension between these competing discourses of marketisation and individual benefit on the one hand and that of social responsibility, community engagement and societal benefit on the other (Millican, 2014). Boden and Nedeva, writing in a UK context, and other academics (Newson in Canada and Giroux in the USA) also identify a mismatch between discourses of social justice and the narrowing of a university experience to serve the needs of employers and cast students as consumers. These underlying tensions between social engagement and employability agendas have come to frame many of the recent developments in the university's third mission and SCE in the second decade of the twenty-first century.

References

AGR (1995) *Skills for Graduates in the 21st Century*. Cambridge: Association of Graduate Recruiters.

Barnett, R. (1994) *The Limits of Competence: Knowledge, Higher Education and Society*. Buckingham: SRHE/Open University Press.

Barnett, R. (1997) *Higher Education: A Critical Business*. London: Open University Press with the Society for Research into Higher Education.

Boden, R. and Epstein, D. (2011) 'A Flat Earth Society? Imagining academic freedom', *The Sociological Review*, 59(3), pp. 476–95.

Boden, R. and Nedeva, M. (2010) 'Employing discourse: Universities and graduate "employability"', *Journal of Education Policy,* 25, pp. 37–54.

Boud, D., Keogh, R. and Walker, D. (eds) (1985) *Reflection. Turning Experience into Learning*, London: Kogan Page.

Bourner, T. (2008) 'The fully functioning university', *Higher Education Review*, 40(2), pp. 26–45.

Bourner, T. and Rospigliosi, P. (2008) 'Forty years on: Long-term change in the first destinations of graduates', *Higher Education Review*, 41(1), pp. 36–59

Gibbs, G. (2010) *Dimensions of Quality*. Higher Education Academy.

Giroux, H.A. (2010) 'Public Values, Higher Education and the Scourge of

Neoliberalism: Politics at the Limits of the Social'. At: www.culturemachine. net/index.php/cm/article/viewFile/426/444 [accessed 21 October 2014]

Hague, D. (1991) *Beyond Universities: A New Republic of the Intellect*. London: Institute of Economic Affairs.

HEQC (1997a) *Graduate Standards Programme Final Report: Vol. 1 The Report*. London: Higher Education Quality Council.

HEQC (1997b) *Graduate Standards Programme Final Report: Vol. 2 Supplementary Material*. London: Higher Education Quality Council.

Laredo, P. (2007) *Toward a Third Mission for Universities*, Paper given at a UNESCO research seminar on Main Transformations, Challenges and Patterns in Higher Education Systems. Paris, 5–6 March 2007.

Kolb, D.A. (1984) *Experiential Learning*. Englewood Cliffs, NJ: Prentice Hall.

Newson, J.A. (2004) 'Disrupting the 'Student as Consumer' Model: The New Emancipatory Project', *International Relations*, 18.

Pearson, R. and Baker, F. (1984) *Graduate Supply and Availability to 1986*. Brighton: Institute of Manpower Studies.

Robinson, E. (1968) *The New Polytechnics*. Harmondsworth: Penguin.

Schön, D. (1983) *The Reflective Practitioner*. New York: Basic Books.

Tarsh, J. (1982) 'The labour market for new graduates', *Employment Gazette*, May, pp. 205–15.

Watson, D. (2007) *Managing Civic and Community Engagement*. Milton Keynes: Open University Press.

Willetts, D. (2010) Speech at Universities UH Annual Conference, 9 September 2010, Cranfield University, www.bis.gov.uk/news/speeches/david-willetts-uuk-conference, [accessed March 2014].

Zuber-Skerritt, O. (1992) *Action Research in Higher Education*. London: Kogan Page.

CHAPTER TWO

Influences on the development of student–community engagement

Introduction

This chapter looks at the influences on the emergence of SCE in British universities, taking into account the national historical context and particular national and international movements, as discussed in Chapter One. It looks in more detail at the three parts of a university's mission – teaching, learning and service or engagement, and at how SCE has emerged within a particular historical context. In particular it looks at the influence of the student volunteering movement, the student development movement, service learning as it developed in the USA and science shops as they were developed in Europe. Tracing these earlier influences and how they have contributed to current thinking about SCE serves to link it to and differentiate it from these other initiatives.

Implications of international developments for university education

This chapter sets out to trace the influence of different international move-ments on SCE and student–community research (SCR) programmes in the UK. It supplements Chapter One, which locates SCE within a his-torical context. Together these chapters offer some interesting conclusions:

1. SCE is part of a university's longer history, together
   with the issues of community engagement and social
   justice that have appeared and reappeared in different

periods and in more or less radical guises. They have been prompted by a desire to give service to the community, question privilege and combat elitism, challenge injustice or develop a sense of neighbourliness, or apply research to real-world problems. On different occasions they have been initiated by students, lecturers, university management and national government. The ways in which they have emerged and are articulated tend to be in response to economic, political and institutional pressures. However, involvement with issues outside of academia has always been part of a university's mission.

2. Similarly, the tripartite mission, or the three different concerns of universities – teaching, research and engagement – have also been part of university structure since earliest times, with different elements coming to the fore at different times. What should be taught, and how, has been influenced by changing views on what constitutes worthwhile knowledge and how far graduates are likely to be employed inside or outside of the academy when they graduate.

3. The dominant pressures facing universities currently – needing to act as a market in competing for and retaining student numbers, and having a social mission which prioritises justice, equity, sustainability and social responsibility – are in many ways in tension with each other. Both of these pressures play out in how universities attract their students, prepare them for their future roles as professionals and as citizens, and allocate the income that their being there generates.

4. We are currently on the cusp of a shifting balance of power globally and a similar shift in the status and availability of different forms of knowledge. The respositioning of the West and a challenging of scientific positivism may all have implications for what we understand as the purpose of a university, the status of university-based research and the approaches used in teaching graduates. These will all have implications for how universities and communities work together and the different roles of students, lecturers and researchers.

35

The student volunteering movement

Student volunteering can be traced back to at least the eighteenth century, when religious societies at Oxford and Cambridge Universities were formed by students and their tutors who engaged in visiting the sick and those in prison. As most university students in that century (and the following one) were destined to become ministers of the Anglican Church, this could partly be seen as a form of work experience. The next significant development was the establishment at Cambridge, Oxford, the Scottish universities and the London medical schools of associations of students, with staff support to support overseas missionary work.

During the second half of the nineteenth century, the idealism of university students and some tutors found increasing expression in volunteering at 'home' (i.e. within Britain), particularly within inner cities. This included missionary work, extension schemes and voluntary work in the poorest parts of the larger cities. Students and their tutors set up community centres in the forms of club rooms and coffee houses.

The 1880s saw the start of the university settlement movement, whereby groups of educated men from universities established settlements in the poorer parts of the larger towns to engage in volunteering in the community. The best-known example is Toynbee Hall set up in 1884. University settlements and college missions started homes for working boys, mothers, Sunday schools, clubs for boys and girls, savings banks, cadet corps, sports teams and boys' and girls' clubs. Most of the residents were undergraduates, often working vacations only, and recent graduates. University settlements were established by most of the universities that existed at the start of the twentieth century. Some of these, such as Barton Hill in Bristol, and in Edinburgh, are still in existence today. An article written by Manthorpe in 2001 identifies 157 student-run voluntary action groups in the UK, operating independently of their HE institution and of local voluntary groups. Generally known as Student Community Action groups, they are co-ordinated nationally through Student Volunteering UK (formerly the National Centre for Student Volunteering).

Enthusiasm among students for social service grew during the first decade of the twentieth century and became a significant part of the life of all British colleges and universities in the years before World War I (Brewis, 2010). Student volunteers provided clubs, classes, dispensaries, summer vacations and summer camps and supported maternal and child welfare services, first aid and home nursing. In this period, joint social service committees were formed within Christian societies, the Student Christian Movement (SCM), Fabian societies, social study groups and suffrage societies. By this time it was providing a vehicle for the expression of youthful idealism and social concern. Arguably, the increasing number of women among the student population was a significant factor.

During World War I, much of the impetus to volunteer was drawn into volunteering for the armed forces and to supporting the war effort, for example support for refugees, and after the war students were heavily involved in the post-war relief effort, including, for example, the relief of the post-war famine in Russia. The formation of the National Union of Students (NUS) was partly the result of this effort.

> *Enthusiasm for social service became a unifying interest among students of all religious and social backgrounds in the years before and during the World War I. To attend an HE college before 1914 was still a privilege reserved for a small minority in Britain, engendering a strong ethic of service among students. The Student Christian Movement started a Social Study Department to prepare social service text books and in 1909 a Social Service Committee was formed to develop and coordinate this work in colleges and universities across the country. In 1908 a course of lectures on poverty and social service by leading social workers such as Samuel Barnett attracted more than 500 students from the University of London* (taken from www.studentvolunteeringhistory.org/1900-1919.html).

In the 1920s and 1930s many students became involved as volunteers in the new 'work camp movement'. A work camp involved a group of young volunteers working on a practical project such as a community centre or youth hostel. The volunteers were often from different countries and the spirit of internationalism was strong. The NUS saw part of its brief as encouraging a 'social consciousness amongst students' and in 1939 produced a 'social services' supplement to an issue of its journal, *New University*.

During World War II student volunteering was concentrated on supporting the war effort by helping in air-raid shelters, volunteering for jobs in hospitals such as cleaning, running activities for evacuated children, teaching in schools and staffing agricultural work camps, for example. The NUS played an increasingly large role, issuing in 1944 a report proposing a 'Pre-University Year of Social Service' i.e. a gap year of social engagement which would help undermine growing concern about universities as ivory towers and further support the war effort.

After the war there was a shift in student volunteering for community-based work to national or international causes such as CND, Oxfam, War On Want, UN Students Association and Anti-Apartheid. The main reasons seem to have been:

- a strong focus on European reconstruction, particularly with work camps overseas;
- the establishment of the welfare state after 1945 to address issues around poverty within the UK;
- cheaper travel and a growing awareness of global issues, including global poverty; and
- the development of a new model of voluntary placement overseas.

The main theme in this period was a shift from social service to community action, i.e. towards a more political and more campaigning position. In 1968 the National Conference on Student Social Services changed its name to the National Conference on Student Community Action. Earlier forms of student volunteering were criticised as 'do-gooding' and this body shifted from a welfare to a 'social justice' perspective. This was seen as a way of getting more students involved in social issues and those driving change at that time were also for the curriculum to be more linked to local social concerns.

Courses must be related to their social context so that knowledge is not considered an end in itself but essentially as a means of improving the quality of our lives together with those of others in society (NUS, 1970, p. 115).

Important developments in this period included the following:

- Students questioned the value of the HE provided by universities and colleges, with greater emphasis on critical thinking leading to criticism of their own higher education.
- Student community action (SCA) groups were established in many HE institutions. This signalled a shift from

service-orientated volunteering such as decorating, mental health work, support for Shelter and teaching immigrants to a more radical campaigning stance on issues such as squatting, campaigns against cuts to public spending, anti-recruitment to the armed forces, anti-racism, alternative education and the development of radical media.

- By the late 1970s internal conflict between those who favoured community service and those favoured a more militant form of community action and also a criticism of these:

    Students' involvement in community action was however controversial during the 1970s, as critics (such as Holden) questioned the legitimacy of students' involvement on the grounds that they did not experience the continual poverty of the residents in the areas where they operated. (Brewis, 2010, p. 6)

- In 1978, financial support from NUS for student community action ended after a financial crisis in the NUS (following the demise of NUS Travel). Finally, at the very end of the 1970s, the Student Community Action Resource Programme (SCARP) which had been established by the NUS collapsed, leaving no national body to support student volunteering focused on either student service or community action.

The key themes in the 1980s were greater involvement of government in seeking to encourage student volunteering, and rising unemployment, particularly youth and graduate unemployment. Significant milestones in this period were:

- After the collapse of SCARP the government funded a Student Community Action Development Unit (SCADU), via the Voluntary Services Unit of the Home Office, to encourage and support student action groups and other volunteering by students.
- In this period the SCA groups tried to get college facilities, such as libraries, more accessible to local communities.
- As unemployment rose in the early 1980s, SCA groups often supported local unemployment centres.

- As graduate unemployment rose there was also increasing recognition that student volunteering developed skills that could be valuable on students' CVs.
- During the 1980s there was increasing emphasis among SCA groups on anti-racism, equal opportunities and the rights of people with disabilities.

(See 'Students, volunteering and social action', www. studentvolunteeringhistory.org/1980-1999.html)

The 1990s saw a further shift from volunteering as a grassroots movement to involvement by government. The Conservative Government sought to make membership of the NUS voluntary and at the same time introduced its Make a Difference Strategy in 1994, which heavily funded a National Centre for Student Volunteering in Community. It focused on training for volunteering, good practice in volunteering, new group development and promoting student volunteering nationally and locally.

This period can be seen as the beginning of 'mainstreaming' of student volunteering rather than grassroots student initiatives. The mainstreaming approach was supported by the Labour Government that came to office in 1997 and was part of its 'active citizenship' initiative, introduced in response to declining rates of student voting. In 2000 the National Centre for Student Volunteering was developed into Student Volunteering UK (subsequently split into Student Volunteering England and Student Volunteering Scotland). In 2001, the first national Student Action Week was initiated to coincide with the launch of the UN's International Year of the Volunteer. In 2002, a new Higher Education Action Communities Fund (HEACF) made £27 million available to UK HE institutions to promote and support various forms of student volunteering. It shifted the centre of gravity further from student-led SCA groups linked to a particular institution's student union, to an institution's administrative structure, including voluntary placements through its employability unit or as part of academic modules. HEACF funding also created and supported hundreds of paid volunteer co-ordinators. In 2009 the vinspired students project was established by the National Co-coordinating Centre for Public Engagement, to focus on identifying the impact of volunteering on communities, institutions and the students themselves (www.publicengagement.ac.uk/about/vinspired-students).

Considerable resources had been committed to promoting and supporting student volunteering in the 2000s but the banking-led recession of 2008 and the subsequent Coalition Government's commitment to public spending cuts meant much of the funding disappeared. This coincided with Prime Minister Cameron's vision of a 'Big Society', committed to volunteering and the rhetoric of neighbourhood-led community work. It became clear that it was necessary to find ways of mainstreaming student volunteering, including student action, if it was not to become subject to the vagaries of unstable government funding allocations. Developing SCE within the HE curriculum offered a potential way of mainstreaming it (Sodha and Leighton, 2009). However, the NUS view shifted during this time from being generally positive about curriculum related to social action in the 1970s, to seeing this as an attempt to introduce compulsory volunteering and contrary to the real spirit of the volunteering movement. It is now in the process of shifting again as the NUS collaborate with Cameron's Big Society Community Organisers' Programme to employ organisers within the NUS as part of their We are the Change campaign. They see this as a vehicle to stimulate voter registration, bridge people together and connect students in a way that enables them to make their voice heard (see Pearce, 2013).

The student development movement

During the first half of the twentieth century, university education in Britain was dominated by the advancement of knowledge part of the tripartite mission, focused on disseminating up-to-date knowledge and developing students' critical faculties. By the 1950s and 1960s there was increasing concern that the goal of a 'rounded education' had been lost. According to Wrenn, 'Institutions of higher education are responsible for developing in their students, essential interpersonal skills and understanding as well civic, vocational and personal knowledge and skills' (1951, p. 25). Ten years later, Mueller (1961) outlined 'three major developmental tasks in the college years: 1) integrating and stabilising the 'self', 2) identifying all the different roles one can play, and 3) practicing and evaluating the activities and attitudes necessary for future roles' (pp. 108–16).

By the late 1970s, models of student development had emerged to support what had become a student development movement. Perry (1968) offered a theory of intellectual and moral development in HE, starting with simplistic forms where students interpret their worlds in unqualified polar terms of good–bad and right–wrong, through to commitment to ideas, values, behaviours and other people in a relativistic world. Astin (1985) offered a theory of 'involvement', including student groups, residential living and community service, in which the institutional environment plays a critical role by affording students a variety of opportunities for encounters with other ideas and other people.

The 1970s and 1980s were the heyday of so-called 'humanistic psychology' with its goal of personal development, self-actualisation and realisation of the fully-functioning person. Rogers' *Freedom to Learn*, originally published in 1969, became increasingly influential and Boyer (1987) wrote, '…the claims of community must be vigorously affirmed. By 'community' we mean an undergraduate experience that helps students go beyond their own private interests, learn about the world around them, develop a sense of civic and social responsibility, and discover how they, as individuals, can contribute to the larger society of which they are part.' (pp. 67–8).

The main themes that emerge from this story of the student development movement are:

- a concern that HE was too focused on conveying knowledge of an academic discipline and developing critical faculties and should include personal and moral development; and
- a concern with self-development, including, for example, gains in self-knowledge and values clarification and with civic and social responsibility and a wider contribution to community and society. The latter included people like Astin and Boyer and has helped to provide the intellectual underpinning for service learning in the USA and SCE in the UK.

Service learning as it developed in America

The incorporation of social action into the curriculum is seen most obviously through the service learning movement in the USA, and has had a significant influence on the development of SCE in the UK. Service learning advocates the use for experiential education for:

- intellectual development;
- cross-cultural awareness;
- civic and social responsibility;
- ethical development;
- career exploration; and
- personal growth (National Centre for Public Service Internships, 1978) and 'a means of gaining a deeper understanding of course content, a broader appreciation of a discipline, an enhanced sense of civic responsibility, and/or a greater interest in and understanding of community life' (Elon University, at: www.elon.edu/e-web/org/sasa/SLResources.xhtml).

These have become recognised as the core principle of service learning. It is worth exploring the history of this movement in the USA and how it developed to become an internationally recognised approach to student action.

Many colleges and universities in the USA were originally established to serve their communities as well as to educate their citizens. The Morrill Act of 1872 donated public lands for sale in each state for the 'endowment, support, and maintenance of at least one college ... to teach such branches of learning as are related to agriculture and the mechanical arts, in order to promote the liberal and practical education of the industrial classes in the several pursuits and professions in life' (Morrill, 1872). Extension classes were an explicit part of the mission of these institutions and the USA also had its own settlement movement. In the early years of the nineteenth century, James and Dewey, from the pragmatism school of education, led an educational reform movement which favoured greater emphasis on moral development that produced tangible results, such as a reduction in poverty and social injustice. Up to this point, the 'service' that universities could offer was largely seen in terms of taking knowledge from the universities to share with those outside, but Dewey developed ideas about thinking and learning which underpinned the modern ideas of experiential learning, and would eventually lead to those within the university learning from their experiences outside of it.

In 1951 President Kennedy established the Peace Corps, which emphasised service and international friendship, and in 1964 President Johnson declared a 'war on poverty' and set up Volunteers In Service

To America. By the end of 1965, thousands of volunteers had served, or were serving, to help low-income families. The first recorded use of the term 'service learning' was in 1966 in a description of a project in Tennessee, and it was later used by Sigmon and Ramsey (1967) to describe the combination of the achievement of tasks that both met a genuine human need and realised conscious educational development. In 1970 Paolo Freire published *Pedagogy of the Oppressed,* which influenced the form of much service learning. It encouraged a critical pedagogy perspective and conscious-raising approach to education and resulted in some movement in the service learning community from social service towards a more radical stance.

In 1979 the National Student Volunteer Programme became the National Centre for Service-Learning and the *Synergist* published the so-called 'three principles of service learning': (1) those being served control the services provided, (2) those being served become better able to serve and be served by their own actions and (3) those who serve also are learners and have significant control over what is expected to be learned. The National Youth Leadership Council (NYLV) was established in 1983 to prepare future leaders and was the first national body to promote a new vision of learning for college-aged students.

By the early 1980s it was apparent that service learning worked in a practice in a wide range of situations and contexts, but it wasn't yet clear how it did so. Freire's *Pedagogy of the Oppressed* offered a radical theory for this but there was still a sense of theory lagging behind practice. Dewey's theories of thinking and learning and Lewin's theories of action research for addressing social issues offered some insight, as did Revans's theories of 'action learning', developed in the UK, but what was needed was a theory of the process of learning from service. This began to emerge with Kolb's *Experiential Learning: Experience as the Source of Learning and Development* (1984), which had a significant impact on the theory and practice of informal education, adult education, reflective learning, lifelong learning and service learning. At the same time, Schön helped provide a theoretical underpinning for the processes of reflection in learning (see Argyris and Schön, 1978).

From this point onwards the pace of growth of service learning in the USA accelerated. In particular, the initiative shifted from being a grassroots-led phenomenon to national initiatives. Three examples should suffice to illustrate this development:

- In 1985 National Campus Compact was formed as a collection of university and college presidents to help students develop the values and capabilities of citizenship through participation in community service and public service more widely.
- In 1985 the National Association of Service and Conservation Corps was formed and from its early days it stared to add human service projects to the conservation projects.
- In 1985/86 Youth Services America was formed, which included a commitment to service learning.

At the end of the 1980s, the Wingspread Conference (1989) published *Principles of Good Practice in Combining Service and Learning* and President Bush established the Office of National Service to support service initiatives. During the 1990s American colleges and universities took service learning seriously. In 1994 the *Michigan Journal for Service Learning* (later retitled the *Michigan Journal for Community Service Learning*) was set up as the first refereed journal of service learning. Other journals such as the *Journal for Higher Education, Outreach and Engagement* (1996) and the *Journal of Public Outreach* (also 1996) soon followed. In 1996 Boyer published *The Scholarship of Engagement*. It seems reasonable to conclude that by the end of the 1990s, service learning had been mainstreamed in US HE:

- In 1997 the American Association for Higher Education (AAHE) published an 18-volume series of monographs titled *AAHE Series on Service-learning in the Disciplines*. This was significant as the disciplinary context was important in interesting lecturers and professors in the new pedagogy.
- In 1999 the President of *Campus Compact* issued a statement 'in response to alleged concern about the disengagement of college students from democratic participation'. The statement was titled 'The President's Fourth of July Declaration on the Civic Responsibility of Higher Education' and it challenged HE to re-examine its public purposes.
- In 1999 the Wingspread Conference issued a 'Declaration on Renewing the Civic Mission of the America Research University'.

In 2000 a university reform commission on the 'The Future of State and Land-Grant Universities' published its conclusions in a report titled 'Renewing the Covenant: Learning, Discovery and Engagement of a New Age and a Different World', and in 2001 the First International Conference on Service-Learning Research was held, which represented a form of integration of the traditional university focus on the advancement of knowledge and the fact that service learning had entered mainstream university education. Many of the UK programmes (specifically CUPP in Brighton, which received its original funding from the USA) have learned a lot from the US model and the term is still used to describe work in certain UK universities). It is also used as a term extensively in South Africa and throughout Europe.

Most recently there has been increasing emphasis on service–user empowerment and learner participation. There also seems to have been some movement to re-badge 'service learning' as 'community service learning', with a shift towards a rights-based approach. In the latter form, it is more difficult to distinguish community service learning in the USA from SCE in Britain, and even in the USA service learning practitioners have begun to abandon the 'service' terminology, and replace it with 'engaged research' and 'engaged learning' (as observed in the Winona State University Campus contract). The description of the goal of engaged scholarship was 'not to define and serve the public good directly *on behalf of* society, but to create conditions for the public good to be interpreted and pursued in a collaborative mode *with* the community'. The notion that locally generated knowledge should be valued alongside academic knowledge – and student benefit alongside community benefit – is beginning to underpin a broad range of engagement programmes.

Science shops of Europe

While service learning and SCE contribute to the teaching element of the tripartite mission, science shops work through engagement to contribute to the pursuit of knowledge. Developed in northern Europe during the 1970s they involve students working in partnership with civil organisations to research problems of local social concern:

> *They became access points to which local community members or*
> *pressure groups could bring research issues that students would*

take up on their behalf. Many of these were extended to form undergraduate or Master's dissertation projects. By bringing together the energy and initiative of a student with the experience of a community group and the expertise of an academic supervisor, they have been able to add scientific evidence to significant local issues. They have expanded from the hard sciences to include the humanities and soft sciences and are able to provide valuable research information for community groups while offering a significant learning opportunity in interpersonal skills, local politics and applied research. During the past five years they have been re-emerging, supported by the Living Knowledge Network. (Millican and Bourner, 2011, p. 93)

Science shops originated in the Netherlands in the 1960s and 1970s and in Canada in the 1980s, and were initially concerned with making scientific knowledge available for the benefit of groups who could not otherwise pay for this. The first group emerged from within the university system, formed by progressive staff members working alongside activists involved in contemporary student movements. Centred mainly on the hard sciences, science shops would offer to research, for example, the potential impact on air quality of a new factory or the levels of pollution in local water sources. Many set themselves up as small informal consultancy shops committed to responding to issues raised by the local community.

Their ethos was to respond to research problems, rather than generate research questions. However, requests for research lagged behind the kinds of issues that they, as scientists and academics, were interested in, and many began to hand over community generated questions to their students. A professional mediator became necessary to translate a community request into a researchable question, identify the discipline area best placed to address it, and farm it out to students working under a supervisor. This brokering role and the ability to manage both the information needs of the group and the learning needs of students became crucial to the success of science shop projects (Farakas, 2002).

In the late 1970s and early 1980s the availability of generous student grants and the potential to combine Bachelor's and Master's degrees (that students could complete over many years, graduating as and when they were ready) provided a flexibility that is now seldom available. Without having to worry about earning an income, students in the Netherlands could submit a thesis when they were ready and were not bound by an academic timetable. Many took the opportunity to undertake research for community groups. On the whole they acted for, rather than with, these groups in order to maintain an independent scientific voice in what could become a polarised situation between community and industry or activist group and government.

A second wave of science shops in the 1980s was strongly interwoven with the further institutionalisation of alternative movements like the *Bürgerinitiative* in Germany. These were civil society groups, based outside academia, that needed to develop their knowledge base and sometimes turned to universities for assistance. Some of these groups recruited membership among students and university staff members. The key difference from the university-based science shop was that the request for research was formalised and commissioned from outside the university and the power locus was shifted from it being a university initiative to a university response.

A third wave during the late 1990s was based more on a partnership model and was concerned with building up longer-term relationships between the university and other civil society groups; and CUPP, emerging in 2003, is one example of this. However, managing equal relationships between a university and its community is not easy and partnerships struggled with understanding and brokering these new relationships. The development of community-based research as a methodology was a useful tool in helping to understand and work through inequalities in power relationships and the unfamiliar language and culture of the different groups (Millican, 2007). Community stakeholders and academics became jointly involved in planning the research, in the various stages of conducting it, and in the dissemination of its results with community stakeholders involving the co-construction of knowledge.

In the UK, science-shop-related initiatives tend to be rooted in social rather than political activism, and stressed a co-operative approach (finding solutions that will suit everyone and therefore work) rather than oppositional approach (challenging dominant powerful or political groups) (Boothroyd and Fryer, 2004). However, although Dutch science shops have always led the field they continue to seem less comfortable with a partnership approach to working (Farakas, 2002) and the emphasis on students performing original research keeps them from experimenting more with client involvement in research. As pressure increases for students to complete their studies in fewer years, they are discouraged from taking on projects that might prolong the research process. Alongside this a concern with attaining high grades and a subsequent tendency to 'play it safe' can stifle attempts at methodological and theoretical innovation that might come through working in partnership.

More recently, in emerging societies in Eastern and Middle Europe, and in post-apartheid South Africa (Mulder *et al.*, 2001), science shops have sprung up, supported by the Living Knowledge Network (www.livingknowledge.org) and often in partnership with similar institutions in the West. In theory the local academy is in a position to play a significant role in capturing and developing local knowledge and researching, interpreting and sharing local solutions. However, local views of democracy and equality and the status given to academics may make such collaborations difficult. In emerging societies particularly, academics are often seen as authority figures, possessing a form of decontextual knowledge that is far superior to local understandings of context. Effective partnerships based on mutual benefit depend on different forms of knowledge being equally valued and exchanged.

In Europe the structure of university curricula via the Bologna process has become more tightly specified and aligned. As a result, those students working to European standards may have less time and freedom to respond to local initiatives and to apply their research to local issues. This can threaten the availability of students to work alongside and at the pace of community organisations.

Fisher *et al.* (2004) identify four factors influencing the degree and the form of co-operation between science shops and civil society organisations:

1. The condition of civil society and the NGO community
2. Political culture and public discourse
3. Resources
4. Science policy

These could form useful benchmarks for assessing the potential of new science shops in emerging societies.

In the UK, science shops have been established at Queen's University Belfast and the University of Glamorgan in Wales. CUPP's Student Community Research (SCR) programme (discussed in Chapter Seven) operates similarly and links postgraduate students with requests for research from the local community and supports them in taking these on as part of their final dissertation. However, different interpretations of the nature of research between the academy and community partners mean that careful brokerage and negotiation is crucial. In many cases communities understand research very differently from how it is used in the academy and often require a positive evaluation that can be produced for funders rather than a critical overview of an initiative or programme, expecting a very different report than one that might be submitted for an academic qualification. These issues are explored more fully in Section Two of this book.

References

Argyris, C. and Schön, D. (1978) *Organisational Learning: A Theory of Action Perspective*. New York: McGraw-Hill.

Astin, A. (1984) 'Student involvement: A developmental theory for higher education', *Journal of College Student Personnel*, 25(4), pp. 297–308.

Boothroyd, P. and Fryer, M. (2004) 'Mainstreaming Engagement in Higher Education: Benefits, Challenges and Successes', paper presented at the UNESCO Forum Colloquium on Research and Higher Education Policy, Paris, 1–3 December 2004.

Boyer, E.L. (1996) 'The scholarship of engagement', *Journal of Public Service and Outreach*, 1(1), pp.11–20.

Brewis, G. (2010) 'From service to action? Students, volunteering and community action in mid-twentieth-century Britain', *British Journal of Educational Studies*, 58(4), pp. 439–49.

Brewis, G. (2013) '"Towards a new understanding of volunteering in England before 1960?" Back to Basics' Working paper, Institute of Volunteering Research. London: IVR.

Farakas, N.E. (2002) 'Bread, cheese and expertise, Dutch science shops in Europe, the public as stakeholder', *Science and Public Policy*, 31(3), pp. 199–211.

Freire, P. (1970) *Pedagogy of the Oppressed*. London: Penguin Books.

Kolb, D.A. (1984) *Experiential Learning: Experience as the Source of Learning and Development*. Englewood Cliffs, NJ: Prentice Hall.

Lewin, K. (1946) 'Action research and minority problems', *Journal of Social Issues*, 2(4), pp. 34–46.

Manthorpe, J. (2001) 'It was the best of times and the worst of times', *Voluntary Action*, 4(1). Available at: http://www.ivr.org.uk/images/stories/Institute-of-Volunteering-Research/VA-Documents/VA4_1/article5_manthorpe.pdf [accessed March 2014].

Millican, J. (2007) *Student Community Engagement – A model for the 21st century?* Available at: www.brighton.ac.uk/cupp/images/stories/Static/ student_community_engagement/papers_reports/JM_Bournemouth_07. doc [accessed March 2014].

Millican, J. and Bourner, T. (2011) 'Student–community engagement and the changing role and context of higher education', in T. Bourner and J. Millican (eds) (2011) 'Student learning from community engagement', special issue of *Education and Training Journal*, 53(2/3), pp. 89–99.

Mueller, K. (1961) *Student Personnel Work in Higher Education*. Boston: Houghton Mifflin.

Pearce, T. (2013) '#WeAreTheChange and the importance of community organising'. Available at: www.nusconnect.org.uk/blogs/blog/ tonipearce/2013/11/11/WeAreTheChange-and-the-importance-of- community-organising/

Perry, W.G. Jr (1968) *Forms of Intellectual and Ethical Development in the College Years: A Scheme*. New York: Holt, Rinehart, and Winston (reprinted November 1998; Jossey-Bass).

Revans, R.W. (1983) *ABC of Action Learning*. Bromley: Chartwell Bratt.

Rogers, C. (1969) *Freedom to Learn: A View of What Education Might Become*. Columbus, OH: Charles Merrill.

Sodha, S. and Leighton, D. (2009) *Service Nation*. Demos. Available at: www. demos.co.uk/publications/service-nation [accessed March 2014].

Students Volunteering and Action, Histories and Policies, 1980–1999. Available at: www.studentvolunteeringhistory.org/1980-1999.html [accessed March 2014].

CHAPTER THREE

Making the case for student–community engagement in the higher education curriculum

Introduction

This chapter develops the argument as to why SCE should be a key part of the university curriculum in the UK. It examines in turn each of the main stakeholders of a university: its students, the university as an institution (including its staff) and society more generally and the positive contribution that engaged learning can make to each of these groups, examining their different perspectives in turn. There is increasing recognition world-wide of university-community engagement (Watson, 2007; Watson *et. al.*, 2013) and SCE is an important part of this. As explored in Chapters Two and Three, HE has always had a social dimension that transcends the narrow calculation of private costs and private benefits, and as the market place begins to dominate HE agendas maintaining this is as important as ever. Engaged learning and the facilitation of student experience within local civil society organisations also provides an additional dimension to undergraduate and postgraduate study that is not necessarily subject-centred. It broadens the scope and range of learning outcomes available to students.

The chapter concludes by recommending that all universities should include the opportunity for every undergraduate to study at least one unit of SCE and that this could become a strategic initiative. While engagement should perhaps never be made compulsory, the opportunity for students to take part in social action fulfils an important part of a university's mission.

Background

Subject-centred HE can be defined as a higher education that is focused on equipping students to make a contribution to the advancement of knowledge in their subject of study. Traditionally this has been through the generation, dissemination or deployment of such knowledge which has often been equated with research, teaching or the application of subject knowledge.

Subject-centred HE is often contrasted with student-centred HE, which refers to a higher education that is focused on the advancement of the student rather than their subject of study. This means equipping them to live more successful lives (including successfully finding suitable employment) after they graduate.

There is clearly a measure of overlap between subject-centred and student-centred HE. For example, a student who takes a statistics degree acquires up-to-date knowledge in their field of study, the capacity to apply critical faculties to develop that knowledge, and also the foundations for a career as a graduate statistician. However, there is also a tension, where supporting the advancement of the subject and supporting the advancement of the student pull in different directions. Arguably, that tension has increased in recent decades as expansion of student numbers has meant that the percentage of graduates finding employment in research, teaching or the application of their subject of study has fallen. In 2008, Bourner and Rospigliosi showed that only a few decades ago about two-thirds of all undergraduate students remained in the education system after graduation, and by the early years of the twenty-first century that figure had fallen to less than a third. Furthermore, the stipulation of subject-specific knowledge in graduate vacancies is becoming increasingly rare.

> ... it is also true that every year between 40 percent and 70 percent of all graduate vacancies ask for a degree in any discipline because the knowledge content of the student's degree is immaterial to the position. (Roberts, 2006, p. 12)

In 2008, Bourner and Rospigliosi showed that in the later years of the twentieth century about two-thirds of undergraduate students remained in the education system (in research, teaching or engaged in further academic study) after graduation and by the early years of the twenty-first century that figure had fallen to less than a third.

Student–community engagement as part of a university education

The inclusion of SCE within the undergraduate curriculum can make a positive contribution to *each* of the main stakeholders of a university. Definitions of SCE are included in the introduction to this book but this chapter looks in more depth as the benefits of SCE to each of the main stakeholder groups.

The benefits to students have been seen to be:

- the development of a capacity for *lifelong learning* through reflective thinking, reflective learning and reflective practice;
- the gaining of *self-knowledge*, including knowledge of personal values, aspirations, strengths and limitations;
- the enhancing of *employment prospects* of students, including real-world experience which can improve a CV and confidence in dealing with applications and interviews;
- the opportunity to develop an emotional literacy in dealing with difficult situations; and
- the enhancement of student satisfaction with the university *experience* itself by connecting with a broader range of people and feeling part of the city in which they are living.

Each of these assertions are further developed below.

1. *Learning to learn for lifelong learning.* If the purpose of a university education is to equip students to lead more successful lives after graduation, however they define success, then developing their ability to learn from reflection will contribute to that outcome as reflective learning can make a major contribution to lifelong learning. While professional and vocational courses already include units which help students develop their skills of reflection and reflective learning, many

do not. Reflective learning supports autonomous learning helping people to learn without a programme of study.

2. *Gaining self-knowledge.* SCE programmes allow students to confront their own values and aspirations and how they might realise these in the future. In ancient Greece, self-knowledge was the primary goal in the development of reason, the first injunction being 'Know thyself.' An increase in self-knowledge is an important outcome of SCE which makes it particularly valuable as an option on courses that would otherwise focus on technical skills, abstract thought or knowledge about the material world. It enriches the curriculum and provides emotional literacy for courses that would not otherwise include this. Many technical as well as social projects succeed or fail because of the skills of a project manager in dealing with people.

3. *Graduate employability.* Research has shown that SCE can enhance the CVs of students and hence also their employment prospects (Bourner and Millican, 2011). A significant number of employers prefer a student with some practical experience and evidence of their ability to deal with difficult or challenging situations. In many instances modules provide an opportunity for extending theoretical learning into a real-world context and applying theory to practice. It extends students' awareness of organisations, how they are structured and how they work, deepens students' understanding of how policy works in practice and how policy, practice and theory together influence what happens in the world. In many instances SCE modules can provide a good preparation for a substantial technical placement period or opening up possible avenues for employment in the voluntary sector that others would not have considered before.

4. *Expression of pro-social inclinations.* A recent survey of graduates at Brighton indicated that a large number (45 per cent) arrived with pro-social inclinations (i.e. a concern to be involved with key social issues during their studies [Red Brick, 2013]) and an SCE module offers a means of expressing these. Optional modules, in which students further identify community projects that relate to their personal interests, put more choice in the university curriculum. In other words, SCE can contribute to a university education that is richer, broader and with more opportunities. This is likely to enhance the attraction of a particular

university for a significant number of students, making it a valuable part of a university's offer.

5. *Enhanced student satisfaction.* SCE can also make a significant contribution to enhancing the student experience itself; students choosing an SCE module are likely to become happier because recent research has found that pro-social behaviour enhances happiness (Lyubomirsky, 2007). This is one of the significant findings from the new science of happiness that has developed since advances in brain imaging in the last decades of the twentieth century increased the confidence of psychologists in measuring happiness. Helping others is one of the keys to happiness (Hamilton, 2010) and, like self-knowledge, contributes to the development of emotional literacy.

The second major stakeholder in any university is the university itself as an institution, including the staff it employs. Here are five ways in which SCE can contribute to institutional priorities:

1. It can help a university realise its mission
2. It can enhance relations between a university and its local community
3. It can enhance relations with government, both central and local
4. It can increase student satisfaction and performance
5. It can enhance the university's attractiveness to students from the local community

The following paragraphs develop these assertions about the institutional value of SCE.

1. *Realising the mission of the university.* University mission statements (for example, Brighton, Manchester, York) often refer to the preparation of graduates as future leaders, world-shapers or responsible citizens. There is an implication here that the kind of education a student receives will equip them to make a contribution to the world as a whole. SCE provides a tangible example of applied education that brings undergraduates into direct contact with questions of citizenship and opportunities for leadership.

2. *Improved university–community relationships.* It has often been observed that US universities enjoy better relations with their local communities than UK universities (Watson, 2007). A plausible reason for this is that SCE, in the form of so-called 'service learning' is much more developed in the USA than in the UK. SCE offers a path to greater respect and benevolence towards a university by its local community.

3. *Improved university–government relationships.* SCE can also improve relationships with government since the primary purpose of government, national and local, is to serve the interests of society and the community respectively. Government is more likely to be forthcoming if it is apparent that universities are serving the interests of society and the local community rather than just their own particular interests. A university that is clearly serving the local community by a well-developed and well-publicised student–community programme is likely to receive more support from the local authority as well as the local community when, for example, it is seeking planning permissions.

4. *Student satisfaction as a performance indicator.* League tables and student satisfaction tables are increasingly important to competing institutions. Experience at Brighton has shown that students on engaged modules record higher levels of satisfaction at the end of their modules, and improved performance on third-year modules, after community-based study. This tallies with research at US universities that shows how service learning modules have increased student performance on other elements of their study. Despite the additional time often taken up by community projects, US research shows students perform better on almost all measures of student outcomes, including, for example, subject knowledge, enthusiasm and enthusiasm for their subject (Burack *et. al.*, 2010, Contis *et. al.*, 2010; Deeley, 2010). Like student satisfaction, these indicators of student performance directly affect assessment of a university's achievement and its position in university league tables and indirectly affect university funding and attractiveness to new students, nationally and internationally.

5. *Enhanced attractiveness to student applicants from the local community.* SCE can enhance the attractiveness of a university to students from the local community as it raises the profile of the institution among groups who otherwise have never considered a university might be for them. This

is particularly the case when SCE involves activities with local schools and colleges. With the large rise in the student fees for an undergraduate course, it is likely that many universities will draw an increasing proportion of their students from the local community, making this a factor of growing importance. Research in Brighton (Millican, 2014) found that even among students paying the highest fees and facing the greatest personal debt, a proportion were interested in courses that provided experience outside the academy, offering the opportunity to learn about sustainability, equity and human rights.

The third major stakeholder in a university is society as a whole and the community in particular. Traditionally, universities have benefited this group in two main ways:

1. They have contributed to the advancement of knowledge through its accumulation, dissemination and application. For most of its history, humankind, like other animals, has been plagued by two great curses: starvation and disease. The accumulation of knowledge has made a significant contribution to increasing food production, material standards of living and the alleviation of disease. The process of natural selection depends critically on *competition*. By contrast, the accumulation of knowledge has been *co-operative*; transcending national boundaries and involving global co-operation. It was probably the first occasion on which humans consciously co-operated on a species-wide basis. It could be argued that the accumulation of knowledge is the primary cause of the great transformation of humankind (Bourner, 2013) and universities have played a significant part over the last 200 years in the accumulation of knowledge. However, it has at the same time led to the global problems of the twenty-first century, environmental degradation and internal conflict over limited resources. These are the challenges currently facing both the hard and the soft sciences.

2. Universities have produced graduates who have contributed to social and material well-being. The medieval university served the Church in individual

spiritual renewal of its populace and in reducing war
and conflict. Graduates from the Renaissance and early
modern university were seen to have had 'a civilising
influence' in what were still 'barbaric times' (Pinker, 2011).
The modern university still produces graduates who can
sustain the material well-being of society by developing a
knowledge-based economy and question the hegemony
of dominant regimes. University students have played a
key role in the uprisings in Iran in 2009 and in Syria in
2011–14.

Universities also make an economic contribution to their environment.
Students bring revenue to an area, and many choose to stay in the local
area after graduation and make a significant contribution to the cultural
life of the city. New university centres (such as Hastings, as part of the
University of Brighton) have been established in areas in order to make
a contribution to its regeneration. SCE is an integral part of this and can
benefit local communities in a number of ways. Below are five examples:

1. The contribution of students' *time and energy* to complete
   local projects through SCE
2. The contribution of students' (particularly postgraduate
   students') *knowledge and intellect* to research local issues and
   solve local problems
3. The development of students' capacity and inclination to
   contribute to the community after graduation
4. The development of a *sense of social responsibility* and
   citizenship in the next generation
5. A *greater sense of connection* between the institution and
   local people generally, turning it from something that
   people are in conflict with to a place that people might
   aspire to and access of their own accord

These can be substantiated as follows:

1. *The contribution of students' time and energy.* A 20-credit module in SCE
from the University of Brighton generally generates 50 hours of contact
within a local group. Currently there are 500–600 students taking these
modules, generating around 12,000 hours of community activity per

year. This is without counting bespoke modules designed, for instance, to build a website, design a mobile phone app for a local charity, or link social work students to local organisations as part of a formal work placement. Regular evaluations of community partner responses stress the energy and enthusiasm that students bring when compared to many of their regular volunteers. Their time makes a substantial contribution to the local voluntary sector economy which, at a time of austerity, is sparse. US partners have suggested approaching the council to provide free bus travel for students in return in acknowledgement of their impact on local services that the council would themselves otherwise be responsible for (CUPP Futures research, awaiting publication, 2014).

2. The contribution of *students' knowledge and intellect* again makes a valuable contribution to the voluntary and public sector economy. Increasingly at the University of Brighton we are approached by local organisations to research or evaluate services which local organisations would not otherwise be able to fund. Voluntary organisations are currently required to bid competitively for funds in the UK, and to provide evidence of the impact of their work. Research or evaluations supported by a local university carry significant weight in proving the value of their work, and well-supported, carefully designed research projects can enable an organisation to both gain funds and to use them effectively. The science shop movement in the Netherlands has provided many examples of research carried out on behalf of civil society groups that has defended citizens' voices against those of business in local planning issues, and projects in the USA have been able to prove the innocence of wrongly convicted prisoners in cases they would not otherwise have been able to fund. With the removal of much legal aid in the UK the Innocence project could provide an important model for university-led law clinics for prisoners with no independent means.

3. *Capacity and disposition towards lifelong pro-social behaviours.* Students who participate in SCE are more likely to engage in pro-social activities when they have graduated. This statement is based on research on service learning in the USA (Eyler and Giles, 1999; Brewis *et al.*, 2010). Many students, particularly those from wealthy backgrounds, have had their eyes opened to social injustice and the causes of social injustice by their experience of SCE. University students are disproportionately

from private schools and middle-class environments (Reay *et al.*, 2010). SCE offers a way of affecting the attitudes, beliefs and inclinations of the most well-resourced and influential sector of society in ways that will support pro-social actions after graduation. Exposure to this while a young adult has been shown to directly affect behaviour in later life (see Stoecker and Tyron, 2009).

4. *Social responsibility*. For most of its history the university has accepted responsibility for the 'moral' instruction of its students. However, this held lower priority in the nineteenth and twentieth centuries with the dominance of scientific knowledge, which was difficult to reconcile with the values of objectivity, impartiality and disinterested empiricism, and the rise of logical positivism which denied that questions of morality were even meaningful. In a postmodern age, SCE raises questions of social justice, moral choices and ethical decisions that does not involve moral *instruction* per se but does not avoid these questions. It connects students with the rights and responsibilities of citizenship. The EU's new Framework Programme for Research and Innovation has a focus on societal challenges and outlines many of the dilemmas today's graduates need to get to grips with in the future in terms of future citizenship responsibilities. These include health and well-being, food security, climate change, democratic representation, energy production, transport and inclusivity (see: http:// ec.europa.eu/programmes/horizon2020/en/news/horizon-2020 -brief-eu-framework-programme-research-innovation).

5. *A greater sense of connection between the university and the local community* can mean improved local relationships. The massification of HE and large numbers of students moving into an area and renting property can have a negative effect on the local population (Smith, 2008). Young people leaving home for the first time, living in high density student areas and free of parental responsibility rarely take their neighbours' needs seriously in terms of noise, rubbish and making a contribution to the local environment. Conflict between local communities and student populations is increasingly common and as a transient population who disappear for large sections of the year they make little contribution to local schools or local groups. Without attempts to connect with the local community it is easy for them to resent the university rather than to see it as something they might participate in and gain from. A successful

SCE programme makes and develops these connections and can improve relationships significantly on a neighbourhood level.

The previous section looked at the benefits of SCE in relation to different stakeholder groups. Experience shows that there are also a number of generic advantages, which are equally valuable for all groups:

- It offers a means whereby students of one subject discipline can meet and engage with students from other subject disciplines in the context of academic study and community-based projects.
- It connects the university with the wider community in ways that can increase participation and lead to possible longer-term research partnerships.
- It can provide enhanced job satisfaction and job enrichment for those staff with the most well-developed pro-social leanings.
- Past students are also stakeholders in the university and SCE can be a source of pride to them about the university they attended. This, in turn, can make them more inclined to support their old university.

Obstacles and challenges

Despite the strong case made above for the inclusion of SCE in the HE curriculum, some of the US research cited has also been critiqued (Stoecker, 2014) and there are a number of obstacles and challenges that relate in particular to work in UK universities. This section examines some of these issues.

1. *Institutional conservatism.* Universities can be conservative institutions. According to a former president of the University of Chicago, Robert Hutchins:

> *Every advance in education is made over the dead bodies of 10,000 resisting professors* (Robert Hutchins, quoted by Noble, 1994, p. 63)

Much has changed over the decades since that statement was made and universities are probably rather less conservative now than they were then. But changes to the curriculum content or teaching and learning methods in response to a changing world often meet stiff resistance. University staff often reflect the culture of the environment and the pool of graduates they draw from and rural or traditional institutions tend to be more conservative that more diverse city-based environments or newer institutions.

The particular conservatism that impedes the development of SCE in HE is associated with nostalgia for the subject-centred education that dominated universities in the later years of the twentieth century. For many university academics who currently hold senior positions, this is what constitutes a 'proper' university education. In most subjects, this is an education focused on up-to-date knowledge of a field of study and the application to it of well-honed critical faculties. Many of those more senior academics will have been sceptical about the calls to modify university education to support graduate employment from the 1980s onwards, and sceptical also of the calls for changes to university education to support lifelong learning from the 1990s. Some of them are sceptical now about broadening the curriculum of a university education further to include a society-centred part in the form of SCE within the undergraduate curriculum.

It is instructive to observe how much easier it appears to have been to introduce SCE in the form of service-learning into the undergraduate curriculum in the USA. What is the difference that has made the difference? Perhaps the main difference is that the undergraduate degree in US universities is viewed as a comparatively broader higher education with study for a Masters degree seen as the professional level of HE where the more focused subject specialisation takes place. American students *major* in a particular field of study which leaves a large minority of the undergraduate programme for other studies, including SCE as service-learning.* By contrast, undergraduate education in the UK is more specialised, attempting to realise a professional level of understanding of a student's subject of study by the time students complete their first degree. This means that the undergraduate curriculum in most UK universities is more specialised, more congested and more resistant to

---

* It helps, too, that typically school-leaver entrants to US universities are a year younger than their UK counterparts and that the full-time undergraduate degree in the USA is typically four years compared with three years in the UK. This creates more space within the undergraduate curriculum.

the inclusion of further elements that are not subject-centred (Dalley, *et al.*, 2008).

There is, nevertheless, considerable evidence of the broadening of the undergraduate curriculum in the UK from the 1980s onwards (Bourner, 2004). This is likely to move the UK undergraduate education towards the US model with the more intense subject specialisation pushed up to Masters courses as the professional level of HE. This will facilitate the adoption of SCE within the undergraduate curriculum. Advocates of SCE can therefore encourage the realisation of their goal by supporting a vision of university education in which specialisation to professional level takes place at Masters level. The case for such a vision has been greatly enhanced by the rise in HE participation rates over the last few decades but the current rise in UK tuition fees is already having an impact on registration for Masters programme and the future is currently uncertain.

2. *SCE takes time, money and commitment, resources which may be in short supply.* Introducing and managing an SCE programme is time intensive. To deliver it properly students should be in small groups, with a level of trust between them and the ability to work openly with each other and their tutor. The personal development element that comes from working in challenging circumstances can require more face-to-face tutorials or enquiries and uncertainties that cannot always be dealt with in class time. Identifying and managing relationships with community partners, responding to requests for community projects and brokering those projects in order to ensure they are safe and reliable is an administratively heavy process, requiring either close collaboration with a volunteering or placements unit or additional administrator support. Students may ask for travel expenses to get to out of town locations and whether these are paid by the community partner or the university these need to be negotiated and agreed. Real projects are harder to control than fictitious scenario exercises and are often run over the time allotted by the university calendar, with a subsequent impact on exam board process and the administration around this. Staff taking on the coordination of SCE programmes may need additional time to manage these than that required by a traditionally taught university based module.

3. *Student–community engagement as an unfamiliar pedagogy.* HE at the undergraduate level has traditionally been based on the dissemination of

propositional knowledge. This was true of the Church-based curriculum of the medieval university, it was true of the classics and humanities-based knowledge of the Renaissance and early modern university, and it was true of the modern university that emerged from Humboldt's ideas in the nineteenth century. In the case of the last of these, critical thinking has been elevated to a pre-eminent position. For example, in 1991, Sir Douglas Hague, chair of Britain's Economic and Social Research Council (ESRC) for most of the 1980s, affirmed that the ability to assess ideas and evidence was the acid test of higher education at a university:

> *Academics must believe that acquiring the ability to test ideas and evidence is the primary benefit of a university education.* (Hague, 1991, p. 64)

SCE values critical thinking too. But it also values strategic thinking and reflective thinking. Mostly, it values learning how to make a difference and that requires strategic thinking, i.e. learning how to be goal-directed and how to realise those goals. It turns out that critical thinking and strategic thinking are both questioning approaches albeit employing different questions. This issue is explored in Chapter Four of this book. Learning to make a difference depends also on the quality of reflective learning and hence also reflective thinking. This is also questioning approach with a further set of key questions and this too is explored in Chapter Four. Lewin suggests that facilitating learning is key to resolving social conflict, enabling individuals to understand and restructure their perceptions of the world around them and encouraging students to take a questioning approach to reflection enables them to rethink the systems they are part of (Burners, 2004).

The upshot of this is that SCE involves a pedagogy which is unfamiliar to many subject-centred academics. Most university academics have been schooled in a pedagogy and epistemology based on propositional knowledge and critical thinking. These academics are less familiar with the epistemology underpinning experiential knowledge and reflective thinking which characterises learning from SCE. This limits of the number of university academics who can deliver SCE and who can assess it.

This raises the question of whether some universities have the capacity to deliver and assess SCE. Fortunately, this is an area where universities are changing. Recent decades have seen a veritable revolution in reflective learning in UK universities (Bourner, 2013). One important factor has been the professional development of university teachers.

Until relatively recent times, and in contrast to school teaching for which new graduates were expected to undertake a course of postgraduate training, it was believed that teaching in a university required no training at all. This was presumably based on the belief that studying at university is more autonomous and self-directed so that teaching university academics to direct and manage their students' learning is unnecessary and possibly even counter-productive. By the end of the 1980s, it was apparent that new technologies for teaching, particularly those associated with the emergent internet (often referred to then as the 'information superhighway') meant that, in future, university teachers would require training and development. Also, the consensus about what constitutes a university education had been broken by such factors as high unemployment of new graduates leading to increasing pressure on university academics to teach skills for graduate employment. 'Employability' and 'work-readiness' were increasingly discussed and it was hard for university academics to argue that graduates should *not* be employable when they graduated, or ready for work when they left university. This, too, had implications for the training and development of university teachers.

Consequently, in the 1990s educational development units★ were established or expanded in universities to provide professional development for new university teachers and also provide continuing professional development for more experienced university academics. This had the effect of bringing more practitioners into university teaching and, consequently, practice-based thinking, blurring the boundaries between academics and practitioners. This was bolstered by the absorption of the polytechnics into the university sector in 1992 as educational development was more developed in the polytechnic sector.

The growth of professional development for university teachers is a crucial part of the reflective learning revolution in university education. Most of the courses of professional development offered by these units were underpinned by the theories developed by Kolb and Schön (Bourner *et al.*, 2003). This meant that new academics would be exposed to reflective learning (whatever the subject discipline of their prior experience of university education) as a learning method. And

---

★ Aka teaching and learning methods (TLM) units.

this also meant, critically, that they were in a position to assess its value, relevance and applicability to a higher education within the subjects that they taught. Moreover, on the basis of their own experiential/ reflective learning, they would be equipped to deliver it themselves to their own students. It became apparent that new university academics were learning as much from their experience of the methods employed on these courses as the intended learning outcomes that appeared in the course outlines (Bourner *et al.*, 2003). As a result of the growth in the professional development of university teachers in the 1990s, enough university staff acquired the capacity to actually deliver reflective learning to allow its adoption across a range of subjects within university education.

4. *The research on long-term benefits is sparse and research has often been weak.* Stoecker, in an article critiquing the dominant approach of service learning in the USA, claims 'we can find little evidence that students are more civically engaged in any substantial way, and particularly in any politically forceful way (Koliba, 2004; Byrne, 2012), and even the academic benefits are slight (Warren, 2012; Parker-Gwin and Mabry, 1998)'. (Stoecker 2014, p. 2). He advocates replacing the term 'community' with 'constituency' and that of service with 'ally'. He puts forward a model of community-based research in which students work alongside community members to identify problems and look for a way forward, claiming 'theories supporting these (SL) practices are problematic' (Stoecker, 2014, p. 1). O'Connor *et al.*, in looking at how service learning research is conducted, cites the findings of the 4th annual Service Learning Conference in critiquing much of this in 2004, saying much of it was insufficiently rigorous or systematic (Furco, 2005). Stoecker (2010) emphasises how the benefits to communities often claimed are rarely based on evidenced research, as much of this focuses on student outcomes. To really understand the longer-term benefits of SCE to all its stakeholders more research is clearly needed.

5. *Course-based academic structures.* Another reason why SCE (in the form of service learning) has become more developed in the US universities is that undergraduate education in that country is typically based on modular programmes of study. By contrast, in the UK universities the academic course plays a more prominent role in the administrative structures of universities. In many UK universities modularity is only skin

deep. This puts universities in the UK at a disadvantage when compared with their US counterparts in terms of their ability to include SCE.

Conclusions

This chapter has offered a range of reasons for introducing SCE into the HE offered by universities and some of the challenges these present. While it makes a powerful case for the inclusion of SCE as part of university education, there is an acknowledgement of the obstacles that need to be overcome. While it does not currently form part of the descriptors in the UK Professional Standard Framework (UKPSF) for teaching and learning, including it in here may help facilitate its inclusion more generally in university curricula. However, on balance this chapter makes the case that SCE should, in 2014, be seen as an important but optional part of all undergraduate education. In order to do this, institutions need to engage with the deeper values and purposes of SCE and equip staff with the time and resources to deliver it well. The arguments presented in this chapter are stronger for some universities than for others and each institution will need to find a model and a structure that fits with their broader undergraduate offer and the mission statement they have set for themselves. For some it will be an optional and occasional offer and for others it may be central to an approach to teaching and learning. It is possible that a university may wish to develop an undergraduate programme-centred SCE and incorporate experiential and engaged learning into all its learning aims and outcomes. The key issue here would seem to be whether there is sufficient demand for this at student, community and faculty level and whether relationships between the academy and its locality were advanced enough to support it.

References

Bourner, T. (2004) 'The broadening of the higher education curriculum, 1970–2002', *Higher Education Review*, 36(2), pp. 45–58.

Bourner, T. (2008) 'The fully-functioning university', *Higher Education Review*, 40(2), pp. 26–45.

Bourner, T. (2013) '*The Great Transformation*'. Unpublished (available on request from author).

Bourner, T., Heath, L. and Rospigliosi, A (2013) 'The fully-functioning university and its higher education', *Higher Education Review*, 45(2), pp. 5–25.

Bourner, T. and Millican, J. (2011) 'Student–community engagement and graduate employability', *Widening Participation and Lifelong Learning*, 13(2), pp. 68–85.

Bourner, T. and Rospigliosi, A. (2008) 'Forty years on: Long term change in the first destinations of graduates', *Higher Education Review*, 41(1), pp. 36–59.

Brewis, G., Russell, J. and Holdsworth, C. (2010*) Bursting the Bubble: Students, Volunteering and the Community, Full Report*. NCCPE (**v**inspired students), University of Bristol.

Burack, C., Prentice, M. and Robinson, G. (2010) *Assessing Service Learning Outcomes for Students and Partners*, IARSLCE Conference, Indianapolis, IN

Burnes, B. (2004) 'Kurt Lewin and complexity theories: Back to the future?', *Journal of Change Management*, 4(4), pp. 309–25.

Contis, E., Stacey, K. and Petrescu, C. (2010) *Increasing Retention of STEM students*, IARSLCE Conference, Indianapolis, IN.

Dalley, K., Candela, L. and Benzel-Lindley, J. (2008) 'Learning to let go: the challenge of the de-crowding the curriculum', *Nurse Education Today*, 28(1), pp. 62–9.

Deeley, S. (2010) 'Service-learning: Thinking outside the box', *Active Learning in Higher Education*, 11, pp. 43.

Eyler, J. S. and Giles, D. E. Jr (1999) *Where's the Learning in Service-Learning?* San Francisco, CA: Jossey-Bass, Inc.

Hague, D. (1991) *Beyond Universities: A New Republic of the Intellect*. London: Institute of Economic Affairs.

Hamilton, D. (2010) *Why Kindness is Good For You*. London: Hay.

Kerr, C. (1991) *The Great Transformation in Higher Education*. New York: State University of New York Press.

Kotter, J. (1996) *Leading Change*. Harvard: Harvard Business School Press.

Lyubomirsky, S. (2010) *The How of Happiness: A Practical Guide to Getting The Life You Want*. London: Piatkus.

Millican, J. (2014) 'Engagement and employability: Student expectations of higher education', *The All Ireland Journal of Teaching and Learning in Higher Education*, 6(1), pp. 16–21.

Noble, K. (1994) *Changing Doctoral Degrees: An International Perspective*. Buckingham: SRHE and Open University Press.

O'Connor, K., McEwen, L., Owen, D., Lynch, K. and Hill, S. (2011) 'Literature Review: Embedding community engagement in the curriculum: An example of university-public Engagement'. Bristol: National Co-ordinating Centre for Public Engagement.

Pinker, S. (2011) *The Better Angels of our Nature: The Decline of Violence in History and its Causes*. London: Penguin.

Reay, D., Crozier, G. and Clayton, J. (2010) "Fitting in' or 'standing out':

Working-class students in UK higher education, *British Educational Research Journal* 36(1), pp. 107–24. Abingdon: Taylor & Francis.

Red Brick (2013) *Brighton Student's Union Research and Rebranding Project*, internal report.

Roberts, L. (2006) *After You Graduate: Finding and Getting Work You Will Enjoy.* Berkshire: Open University Press.

Smith, D. (2008) 'The politics of studentification and (un)balanced urban populations: Lessons for gentrification and sustainable communities?', *Urban Studies*, 45(12), pp. 2541–64.

Stoecker, R. (2014) 'What if', *The All Ireland Journal of Teaching and Learning in Higher Education*, 6(1).

Watson, D. (2007) *Managing Civic and Community Engagement.* London: Open University Press (McGraw-Hill).

Watson, D. (2011) *The Engaged University: International Perspectives on Civic Engagement.* London: Routledge.

CHAPTER FOUR

The pedagogic case for student–community engagement

Introduction

This chapter is about how students' capacities for learning can be developed through SCE, enabling them to draw maximum benefit from their experience of HE and preparing them for taking greater responsibility for their own learning in the future. By differentiating planned learning and unplanned learning (planned by an instructor or by a student themselves, as against incidental learning that arises from experience) it raises questions about the value and development of both of these areas. It focuses more on the UK context in making a pedagogic case for introducing SCE into the curriculum and looks at the value of experiential learning to the development of notions of citizenship and professionalism. It concludes with some discussion on how to support the transferability of learning from experience to these different fields.

Why SCE is important in autonomous learning

A feature of HE is greater autonomy in learning. Much of the learning in schools involves dependence of school students on teachers. For the most part, teachers specify what is to be learned and how it will be learned, providing students with some subject choice at GCSE level and increased subject choice at tertiary level, but still delivering content that has been nationally pre-determined. In Freirean terms this constitutes a banking model of education (in which content is banked in pupils' heads, where it is stored and may possibly be of value in the future, or what has often been referred to as a 'jug and mug' approach, in which the knowledge of a teacher is poured into the empty 'mugs' of students' brains). Entwistle and Peterson (2005) would refer to it as surface learning, concerned with the memorisation of facts (at GCSE level) without any attempt to distinguish any pattern between the facts, to generate new knowledge or to work with the knowledge gained. This is in contrast to what they refer to as 'deep learning' where the learner seeks to engage actively with the content of the learning, to make connections between new learning and what they know already and to apply that learning to other events in their lives. While surface learning might be useful for recalling new information deep learning implies an intention to integrate new concepts into a learner's broader view of the world.

Unlike schools, where students have a high level of dependency on a set curriculum, HE involves greater learner autonomy and choice. Students are able to choose their subject of study and select the content of their course from those on offer at different universities. As undergraduates, they have considerable discretion over what to read and how much. Increasingly, even lectures are seen as voluntary as lecture notes are published online and assessment is based on a final task rather than regular participation. The final piece of much undergraduate work involves students completing a dissertation or extended project in which they specify what they aim to learn (i.e. their research goals) as well as the specific methods (i.e. research strategy and plan of work). This element of choice and planning increases in postgraduate study, and doctoral study is based entirely on the acquisition of knowledge that is new and original and supported by supervision rather than teaching. Neither students nor supervisors at this level are able to specify in advance precisely what knowledge will be acquired.

There is a clear shift from greater dependency to greater autonomy and increasing responsibility for learning and the degree of learner autonomy is an *indicator* of the level of education. Most lecturers would see their role as developing and supporting a student's responsibility for their own learning as a key ingredient of successful study and of lifelong learning.

> ... *our ultimate goal in higher education must be to encourage students to be responsible for, and in control of, their own learning* ...
> (Zuber-Skerrett, 1992, p. 24)

> *A key factor in the transition to university is the enculturation of new*

students into both the discipline they are studying and effective study practices. Most significantly, students, whatever their chosen discipline, must learn to become autonomous learners. Too often this process is either left to chance or seen as a natural attribute of the higher education learning system rather than a particular skill that must be learnt and can be taught. (Railton and Watson, 2005, p.182)

Neary, in discussing his concept of 'the student as producer' (2010) goes further than this to argue for the necessity of students to develop autonomy and to be able to produce and create rather than learn already organised ideas, if society is to radically change. He refers to Vygotsky's notion of a 'zone of proximordial development' or reaching beyond what they saw themselves capable of achieving, as the true goal of HE.

Vygotsky argues that teaching begins from the student's experience in a particular social context. Pushing that notion to the extreme of its radical logic, he suggests that the social context must be arranged by the teacher so that the student teaches themselves: "'Education should be structured so that it is not the student that is educated, but that the student educates himself" or, in other words, "...the real secret of education lies in not teaching'" (Vygotsky, 1997 in Neary, 2010, p. 5).

The central problem addressed in this chapter is how SCE programmes can support a shift in responsibility for, and development of, autonomous learning. It suggests that SCE programmes, by placing learning in context and providing opportunities for unplanned or emergent learning, can make a significant different to a student's development as an autonomous learner.

The majority of learning in a SCE programme involves learning *from* engagement rather than learning *for* engagement. Generally students are not taught a body of theory in preparation for the practice of engagement but rather they go into the community with some background context and draw lessons from the experience. It follows that the conventional model of learning, where students acquire knowledge at university in preparation for later application in practice, is of less value in SCE than the model that reverses this sequence, i.e. whereby the student distils knowledge from their community-based engagement. Much of what is learned by students in the community is context specific. Such situational knowledge is often of more value in dealing with particular issues in community contexts than the propositional knowledge of textbooks which is often of limited relevance to issues that are local, urgent and require action. Learning as the distillation of situational and personal knowledge has been much explored in recent decades by, for example, David Kolb (experiential learning), Reg Revans (action learning) and Donald Schön (reflective learning). Since the learning is context specific it is difficult to specify in advance *what* will be learned. In this respect, student–community learning is more like doctoral study than conventional discipline-based undergraduate study, i.e. tutors can offer processes to support the acquisition of such knowledge but cannot specify in advance precisely what knowledge will be acquired.

This is valuable in that developing students' ability and disposition to take control of their own learning is important for life after university, where learning is rarely related to instruction. The accelerating pace of change in technology, communication and employment emphasises the need for continued learning beyond initial professional training and this need is escalating. The most valuable preparation a university education can provide may well be developing the capacity to learn how to learn. It matters also for the credibility of SCE itself within the university and within HE more generally. Traditional university values of skepticism and academic scrutiny inevitably raise questions about whether experiential learning provides sufficient opportunity for critical analysis and is appropriate for academic institutions. Developing students' capacity to take responsibility for their own learning is an indicator of its value and its place within the academy.

Planned and unplanned learning

Learning can be partitioned into planned learning and unplanned learning, categories which are both mutually exclusive and exhaustive, and this distinction is helpful in approaching the elements of learning involved in SCE. Understanding these differences affords students more control over the management of them.

Planned learning involves learning that is goal-directed and informed by a pre-specified learning outcome(s) set by either a tutor or the learner themselves. In order to reach the goal some strategy, however rudimentary or complex, is necessary and, for this reason, planned learning can also be termed *strategic* learning. Most formal education is orientated towards goal-directed or strategic learning. It starts with learning outcomes and the educator and/or learner devises ways of realising these. This is not always apparent at the early stages of education because the process is divided; the teacher does most of the planning and the student most of the learning, but it still depends on strategic thinking and the development of a strategy for reaching learning goals. Developing students' powers of strategic thinking would therefore equip them for more control over planning their own learning and their own projects. *Unplanned learning* includes all those areas of learning that are not in response to purposeful movement towards pre-specified goals. Unplanned learning is closely related to experiential learning, emergent learning, informal learning, incidental learning and reflective learning. As such, it includes learning which happens through the experience of life. There is some consensus that it is the process of reflection that distils learning from experience, but it is not a unanimous one. Swan (2005), for example, claims 'Contrary to an assumption widespread amongst educationalists, learning is mostly an unconscious process.' However, within HE a focus on learning that is conscious and deliberate seems appropriate and for unplanned learning that means learning through reflection.

Reviewing an experience is the process of bringing it into awareness, recovering memories of the experience so that it is available for examination or critical analysis. This is the 'data' which is examined using reflective thinking (Bourner, 2010). Developing students' powers of reflective thinking would equip them to take more charge of their own experiential learning, emergent learning, informal learning, incidental learning and reflective learning, i.e. their unplanned learning.

The importance of questioning

To become more autonomous as a learner requires the development of strategic and reflective thinking, and the ability to differentiate these from critical thinking, the dominant approach taught within academia. Critical thinking involves the ability to test ideas and evidence and undergraduate students are encouraged to use searching questions to interrogate the material with which they have been presented in order to develop their own critical thinking skills. The kind of questions used in critical thinking are represented in the list below and can be used in relation to most texts:

1. What *explicit* assumptions are being made? Can they be challenged?

2. What *implicit/taken-for-granted* assumptions are being made? Can they be challenged?
3. How logical is the reasoning?
4. How sound is the evidence for the assertion(s)?
5. Whose interests and what interests are served by the assertions?
6. What values underpin the reasoning?
7. What are the implications of the conclusions?
8. What meaning is conveyed by the terminology employed and the language used?
9. What alternative conclusions can be drawn from the evidence?
10. What is being privileged and what is off the agenda in this discourse?
11. What is the context of this discourse? From what different perspectives can the discourse be viewed?
12. How generalisable are the conclusions?

Just as the process of critical thinking implies asking searching questions of an assertion so the process of strategic thinking implies asking searching questions before a course of action. The kind of questions that can be used to support strategic thinking are shown below.

1. What *precisely* is the goal?
2. What purpose does the goal serve? What values does the goal serve?
3. What are the main obstacles to reaching the goal?
4. Who might already know how to achieve the goal?
5. Who else has an interest in the achievement of the goal, i.e. who are the stakeholders?
6. What are the contexts of the 'project'? Is it part of a larger system?
7. Can the goal be broken down into sub-goals?
8. What are all the possible options?
9. What are the relative merits of the different options?
10. What resources are needed?
11. How can progress be monitored?
12. What evidence could be provided that the goal has been achieved?

In SCE strategic thinking can be used in planning learning or in planning how to achieve a particular outcome on behalf of a community group. Many SCE projects require students to use a creative approach to designing a course of action or resolving a community problem. Being able to use strategic thinking to set goals and to explore alternatives, to interrogate the context and to evaluate progress, is valuable in almost any field of work that involves autonomy and responsibility. As such, it could be seen as a key graduate skill. It enables a student to plan their own learning and to plan what they will do with that learning, to see it within a broader context. Asking questions like, 'What do you see as the main obstacles?' helps the anticipation and management of risk and skilled strategic thinking includes the exploration of alternative ways of achieving learning outcomes.

While critical thinking implies asking searching questions of a text and strategic thinking uses questions to interrogate a future goal, reflective thinking uses questioning to unpack the significance of an experience. Uncritically reviewing or recalling an experience does not constitute reflective thinking; it is equally as possible to review an experience unreflectively as it is to listen to a talk uncritically, and terms such as critical reflection or reflective analysis are used to emphasise this difference. The following list contains the type of questions that support the interrogation of experience:

1. What pattern(s) or themes can you recognise in your experience?
2. What happened that most surprised you? Why did it surprise you? What does that tell you about your prior beliefs?
3. What was the most fulfilling part of it? What does that imply about your values?
4. What was the least fulfilling part of it? And what does that tell you about what you don't value?
5. How do you feel about the experience now compared with how you felt about it at the time? What does that imply about how you've changed?
6. What does the experience suggest to you about your strengths and comparative advantages?
7. What does it suggest to you about your weaknesses and opportunities for development?

8. What did you avoid? What did you risk?
9. What did you learn from the experience about how you react and how you respond?
10. From what other perspectives could you view the experience?
11. What options did you have? Is there anything that you might have done differently?
12. What might you do differently now or in the future as a result of that experience and your reflections on it? What actions do your reflection lead you to?

The three lists show that critical thinking, strategic thinking and reflective thinking all involve asking searching questions. While the questions each involve are different, they all share questioning as their core process and it is this shared process which makes the university's long experience with developing the ability to test ideas and evidence relevant to developing more holistic powers of learning.

The figures that follow illustrate the relationship between questioning styles, process and the competencies developed. Figure 4.1 shows that the ability to test ideas and evidence is based on the ability to think critically which, in turn, is based on the use of questions to interrogate the subject of the critical thinking.

Figure 4.1 Critical thinking as a questioning process

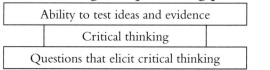

| Ability to test ideas and evidence |
| Critical thinking |
| Questions that elicit critical thinking |

Figure 4.2 shows that the ability to plan and manage learning and to plan and manage creative projects, depends on the ability to think strategically which, in turn, depends on the use of questions to interrogate possible courses of action.

Figure 4.2 Strategic thinking as a questioning process

| Ability to plan and manage own learning |
| Strategic thinking |
| Questions that elicit strategic thinking |

Figure 4.3 shows that the ability to distil lessons for an experience is based on reflective thinking which can be elicited by asking searching questions of the experience.

Figure 4.3 Reflective thinking as a questioning process

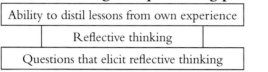

Planned and unplanned learning at the highest level are dependent on the ability to ask searching questions that move from a surface to a deeper level of understanding.

Deep and surface learning and the value of critical pedagogy

The introduction to this chapter looked at the difference between deep and surface learning, indicating that the shift to deep learning was associated with the intention to recognise patterns, to engage directly with the material and to begin to create new meanings from it. In many ways the 'material' used for deep or surface learning can come from text, from plans or from experience, it is possible to identify patterns and to work with meaning in all of these areas. This intention to interrogate, to own and to work with meaning is a crucial part of autonomous learning and a definitive element in HE.

However it also underlies a Freirean definition of critical pedagogy, an approach to education and to learning used initially by Paulo Freire in Brazil to teach literacy to adults who had no experience of formal schooling. Freire's approach to education was essentially political and stems from experience of a particularly oppressive regime in Brazil, from which he was exiled in 1964. He later returned to become minister of education but his early work, outlined in *Pedagogy of the Oppressed* talks about education and the practice of freedom. Freire differentiated between literacy for domestication (learning that involves repetition and following of rules) and literacy for liberation (learning that involves deeper questioning in order to understand context of knowledge and implications for power). Literacy for domestication, banking education or formal schooling in Freirean terms implies being controlled through the selection of the particular forms of knowledge access is given to. The alternative is empowering the learner with the ability to use questions to unpack context, to uncover power relationships and, in some cases, to shift these by broadening access to knowledge. This also resonates with Neary's 'student as producer' discourse which seeks to overthrow traditional power relationships in society through a 'progressive pedagogy (that) involves reinventing the politics of production from within, against and beyond the current social relations of capitalist production' (Neary, 2010, p. 3). Neary links his approach to critical social analysis to Freirean notions of critical pedagogy, claiming that 'pedagogy cannot be "politically indifferent" ... that education follows a basic pattern depending on its dominant social class' (Vygotsky, 1997 in Neary, 2010, p. 6) and that students should be educated to transform their environment rather than adapting to an already oppressive environment.

Critical pedagogy, like deep and surface learning, are important concepts in understanding the significance of SCE and its potential to be more than an instrumental form of education. While the skills associated with it are all valuable to employment, the process of engaging with and interrogating knowledge, and drawing knowledge from experience, enable, in Freirean terms, the ability to challenge oppression. The ability to ask critical questions in an SCE context enables students to question the knowledge they are gaining, the skills they are developing and the impact of their work on the communities with which they engage. It encourages them to see their future aspirations in a broader world context and to question what it is they want to do and to be in the world. This can be unsettling to tutors who are used to maintaining power in a lecture room environment and controlling the pace of learning themselves. bell hooks (1994) describes this process as a willingness to be vulnerable as a lecturer, encouraging students to take risks, to reflect on learning as an individual and to work collaboratively in discovering new knowledge. hooks describes this as 'transformational learning' and draws from Freire's concept of conscientisation – the moment of learning that occurs during a period of vulnerability and deep reflection when learners become aware of their own identity and circumstance. hooks, like Freire, argues that this is the point at which people become aware of the hidden and invisible powers that have limited their lives and start to see themselves as possible agents of change. Both, like Neary, feel this can only happen when students are encouraged to be active 'subjects' in the education process, rather than consumers of other people's knowledge.

Freire's notion of critical pedagogy brings together elements of critical and reflective thinking.

Critical thinking, reflective thinking and strategic thinking share a common two-stage process:

1. Bringing something into conscious awareness.
2. Asking and responding to searching questions.

The literature on higher learning differentiates surface learning from deep learning. Surface learning is associated with uncritical accumulation of facts and opinions and deep learning is associated with critical thinking. Surface learners, like uncritical thinkers, read a text without interrogating it or creating their own meanings, taking it in at face value. By contrast, deep learners, like critical thinkers, personally engage with what they read by asking searching questions of the material. The correspondence between deep/surface learners and critical/uncritical thinkers is equally applicable to the domains of strategic thinking and reflective thinking.

Freire described himself as a curious being. His approach to pedagogy concerns the value of curiosity, a sense of the right to ask deeper questions about how knowledge is constructed as well as about how things work. Students who have been in formal education for most of their lives are often in the habit of accepting rather than challenging the information they encounter. Formal education at secondary level stresses the accumulation of facts and the revision of a preset syllabus, a trend exacerbated by school league tables and a stress on exam results. Students rarely come to university equipped to operate as autonomous learners and many struggle with the lack of structure associated with HE. The process of analysis and interrogation needs to be introduced and the habit of it developed, particularly in the current HE environment where students often see themselves as passive consumers (see Chapter One, section 'The twenty-first century and the neoliberal university'). Regular sessions of question-based discussion, which often appear less on crowded, content driven curricula even at university level, can encourage the habit of asking questions. Claxton (2007) emphasises the distinction between questioning skills and questioning disposition:

> *Asking questions is partly a matter of skill, for sure. One has to know how to formulate good questions ... But 'being questioning' is*

> *also a matter of inclination, of self-confidence, of a sense of occasion,*
> *and of entitlement. It is not much use being able to ask good*
> *questions if in practice you are easily deflected from so doing. Asking*
> *questions makes you vulnerable: it might be a stupid question, or*
> *one to which everyone knows the answer. So the capacity to learn*
> *depends, in part, on being willing to run the risk, and to do so you*
> *need a sense of entitlement: the belief that you have the right to be*
> *curious, to ask questions, to discuss, to imagine how things could be*
> *different.* (Claxton, 2007, p. 6)

When the university took on the advancement of knowledge as its primary goal, it developed the seminar as a way of enabling students to enhance their repertoire of critical questions and practice working with them. However, polytechnics brought with them a different history of preparing students for vocational work which, in many cases, involved learning pre-prescribed ways of doing things. With the incorporation of former polytechnics into university status there has been a merging of both approaches in the new universities that resulted from them, with increasingly crowded curricula and a focus in both institutions of research. Students coming from secondary school expecting to be 'taught' increasingly struggle with seminar-based approaches, and often demand pre-prepared reading lists and a planned learning approach. While the third-year dissertation introduces students to project work and to the notion of choice of unplanned learning, in many universities the focus on autonomy does not really develop until Masters or Ph.D. study. Educationalists, concerned about the disappearance of independent thinking, have sought to address this in different ways.

Neary also argues for the connection of intellectual thought to practical tasks, and defends his notion of student as producer with Vygotsky's 'learning and development approach'.

> *By learning and development Vygotsky does not mean learning*
> *in order to learn, but learning so that the student may develop*
> *intellectually, and emotionally and become more socially aware*
> *(Newman and Holzman, 1993). The learning and development*
> *approach insists that for students to acquire knowledge, the*
> *intellectual function of learning must be associated with practical*
> *tasks.* (Neary, 2010, p. 5)

A key issue for student as producer is that social learning is more than the individual learning in a social context, and includes the way in which the social context itself is transformed through progressive pedagogic practice. Student as producer, Neary claims, is a critical response to attempts by recent governments in the UK, and around the world, to create a consumerist culture among undergraduate students (Neary, 2010).

Healey, on the other hand, promotes the notion of student as researcher and advocates for inquiry-based learning in which students are also active in either supporting or leading a piece of research. Like Neary he discusses the importance of undergraduates becoming active contributors to knowledge rather than passive consumers. He argues for the reshaping of the university with appropriately designed, student-centred approaches to foster deep learning, saying that these approaches should start from the premise that students can be actively involved in the creation of knowledge and that mode 2 knowledge production (Gibbons *et al.* 1994) is blurring traditional divisions between research and teaching. Involving students in research projects or supporting them in the development of their own projects will help them to construct themselves as active learners contributing to the development of knowledge.

Inquiry-based learning and active project work provide *opportunities* for question-based discussion. Action learning in particular offers one practical way to help students develop their strategic thinking and reflective thinking (Lawrence, 1986; Bourner *et al.*, 2000). Action learning provides the opportunity to develop strategic and reflective thinking in the ways that seminars provide the opportunity to develop critical thinking, and SCE programmes often include both action learning sets and reflective blogs. In an action learning set, students ask questions of each other, as they share in a group setting alternative courses for action. Set members also use questions to encourage participants to reflect on the experience of their project and the actions they have taken. Reflective blogs require students to use questions to interrogate their own experience, and by posting this online to encourage comments from their peers. While a traditional university seminar can enable the sort of question-based discussion that supports the development of critical thinking, project work with action learning and reflective writing can provide question-based discussion to support the development of strategic and reflective thinking.

Conclusion: The four domains of knowledge

This chapter has been concerned with the development of planned and unplanned learning, and the role of questioning is to elicit strategic or reflective thinking and to focus thinking. It emphasises the equal importance of different types of thinking and the contribution these can make to achieving personal goals, learning from experience, challenging power structures and making informed decisions. Focused thinking can be forward-looking (and engage the imagination, for example) and backward-looking (and engage the memory). If thinking can be focused through questioning, then deep learning can be seen as the ability to use questions to understand something in depth.

The process of assessment confers legitimacy on learning within a formal educational institution but it is important for assessment to support a learning process rather than to drive it, and this is as true of traditional learning as it is for experiential learning. One approach to assessment of SCE might be to evaluate a student's ability to think critically, strategically and reflectively through the use of searching questions and this is explored further in Chapter Eight.

Bourner's four domains of knowledge (see Figure 4.4) are a useful way to bear in mind the range of knowledge covered by SCE and the kinds of skills developed by it. Grouping these areas between the continuums of knowledge and skills, and internal and external worlds, he locates personal development within the domains of learning and suggests the value of both knowledge about the world and self-knowledge in professional life. Speaking at his inaugural lecture in 1998, Bourner made a plea for the continued inclusion of inner skills and self-knowledge into the HE curriculum and the role of reflective and strategic thinking in developing these areas.

Internal

SCE provides an opportunity to assess critical, reflective and strategic thinking in a way that traditional university education is unable to do. It equips students with skills to manage planned and unplanned learning and, in many cases, sets up a value system that moves them from personal to broader societal goals. It provides an approach to learning that reflects many of the principles of Freirean pedagogy, where students are taught to engage with and to critique their environment and Vygotsky's notion

Figure 4.4 Bourner's four domains of knowledge

External	1 Outer skills e.g. Learning how to play chess e.g. Learning how to drive a car	2 Knowledge about the world e.g. Learning about history e.g. Learning about the theory of managing change in organisations	
Skills			Knowledge
	4 Inner skills e.g. Learning how to manage stress e.g. Learning how to be comfortable making	3 Self-knowledge e.g. Learning about own learning style e.g. Learning about own strengths and weaknesses	
Internal	'cold calls'	as a manager	

of learning and development in which intellectual learning is linked to practical tasks. It incorporates some of Neary's conception of student as producer, where 'Knowledge and meaning are created, and the student is remade, by reconnecting intellectual and manual labour' (Neary, 2010, p.6) and provides a vehicle for students to learn about the world while also learning about themselves.

References

Boud, D. (1988) 'Moving towards autonomy', in D. Boud (ed.), *Developing Student Autonomy in Learning*. London: Kogan Page, pp. 17–39.

Boud, D., Keogh, R. and Walker, D. (eds) (1985) *Reflection: Turning Experience into Learning*. London: Kogan Page.

Bourner, T. (1998) *Bridges and Towers: Action Learning and Personal Development in Higher Education*, Inaugural Lecture, University of Brighton. At: www.brighton.ac.uk/cupp/images/stories/Static/student_community_engagement/papers_reports/assessment.doc [accessed March 2014].

Bourner, T. (2003) 'Assessing Reflective Learning', *Education and Training*, 45(5), pp. 267–72.

Bourner, T. (2004) 'The broadening of the higher education curriculum 1970–2000: An ipsative enquiry', *Higher Education Review*, 36(2), pp. 39–52.

Bourner, T. (2010) 'Reflective learning in HE: Working with experiential data', *Higher Education Review*, 43(1), pp. 21–37.

Bourner, T., Cooper, A. and France, L. (2000) 'Action learning across the university community', *Innovation in Education and Training International*, 37(1), pp. 2–9.

Clark, W. (1989) 'On the dialectical origins of the research seminar', *History of Science*, 27, pp. 111–54.

Claxton, G. (2007) 'Expanding young people's capacity to learn', *British Journal of Educational Studies*, 55(2), pp. 1–20.

Entwistle, N. and Peterson, E. (2004) 'Conceptions of learning and knowledge in higher education: Relationships with study behavior and influences of learning environments', *International Journal of Educational Research*, 41(6), pp. 407–428.

Gibbons, M., Limoges, C., Nowotny, H. and Schwartzman, S. (1994) *The New Production of Knowledge: The Dynamics of Science and Research in Contemporary Societies*. London: SAGE.

Green, V. (1969) *British Institutions: The Universities*. London: Penguin Books.

Green, V. (1974) *A History of Oxford University*. London: Batsford.

Hague, D. (1991) *Beyond Universities: A New Republic of the Intellect*. London: Institute of Economic Affairs.

Healey, M (2010) *The Scholarship of Engagement: A Selected Bibliography*. http://resources.glos.ac.uk/shareddata/dms/98C851E6BCD42A0399FC8C986C5EF7B3.pdf [accessed March 2014].

hooks, b. (1994) *Teaching to Transgress: Education as the Practice of Freedom*. New York: Routledge.

Humboldt, W. v. (1970) 'On the spirit and organisational framework of intellectual institutions in Berlin', *Minerva*, 8, pp. 242–67 (German original, 1810).

Lawrence, J. (1986) 'Action learning – a questioning approach', in A. Mumford (ed.) *Handbook of Management Development* (2nd edn). Hants: Gower.

Leedham-Green, E. (1996) *A Concise History of the University of Cambridge*. Cambridge: Cambridge University Press.

Millican, J. (2007) *Student Learning in the Community. Lessons from Practice*. Brighton: Community and University Partnership Project.

Moore, W. (1968) *The Tutorial System and Its Future*, London: Pergamon.

Neary, M. (2010) 'Student as producer: A pedagogy for the avant-garde; or, how do revolutionary teachers teach?', Learning Exchange, josswin.org

Palfreyman, D. (2001) *The Oxford Tutorial: 'Thanks, You Taught Me How To Think'*. Oxford: Oxford Centre for Higher Education Policy Studies.

Popper, K. (1972) *Objective Knowledge: An Evolutionary Approach*. Oxford: Oxford University Press.

Railton, D and Watson, P. (2005) 'Teaching autonomy: "reading groups" and the development of autonomous learning practices', *Active Learning in Higher Education: The Journal of the Institute for Learning and Teaching*, 6(3), pp. 182–93.

Simpson, R. (1983) *How the PhD Came to Britain: A Century of Struggle for Postgraduate Education*. Guildford: Society for Research into Higher Education.

Swan, J. (2005) 'Learning how to learn', Paper presented to the Educational Research Centre, University of Brighton, 16 March 2005, pp. 1–5.

Tapper, T. and Palfreyman, D. (2000) *Oxford and the Decline of the College Tradition*. London: Woburn Press.

Watson, D. (2007) *Managing Civic and Community Engagement*. London: Open University Press (McGraw-Hill Education)

Wilen, W. (1982) *Questioning Skills for Teachers*. Washington, DC: National Education Association.

Zuber-Skerritt, O. (1992) *Action Research in Higher Education*. London: Kogan Page.

Section Two

Introducing Student–Community Engagement

CHAPTER FIVE

Planning student–community engagement

Introduction

This chapter outlines the key things to consider when introducing a new programme. It involves discussion on how to assess the university context, its mission, purpose, and structure, as well as the community context, such as geography, location of campus, local priorities, and existing relationships with civil society organisations and how the not-for-profit sector is organised. By drawing on the experience of CUPP at the University of Brighton, it provides guidance on questions of outreach, relationship-building and brokering, who to work with and how. It outlines a series of different approaches, depending on internal and external resources and looks at how to identify spaces for civic engagement within the curriculum, student-readiness and staff enthusiasm.

Positioning SCE within the academy

For an SCE programme to be sustainable in the longer term it will need to properly meet the needs of both partners and link to the intentions and the structures of the university, the faculty, the school and the local civil society sector. Reciprocity or mutual benefit are key principles within the majority of engagement programmes, largely because a programme has a better chance of working if both partners are clear about what they are getting out of it. Even the service learning programmes in the USA have on the whole moved away from a service agenda; recognising that the value these programmes bring to student learning is often greater than the contribution they make to their partners (Gelmon *et al.*, 1998). Planning a programme jointly with senior management and local community representatives can help to ensure an ongoing commitment from both sides. In the early days of the Brighton programme discussions about the nature, the shape and the duration of activities were held frequently with community partners.

SCE activities can range from a single project within one taught module, initiated by a lecturer with their own community contacts, to a complex web of engagement activities spread across the curriculum. Table 5.1 provides a framework for deciding where to start.

Table 5.1.

	Group project/s	**Individual projects**
Single module	Where all students from a single module are involved within one community project. Set up probably through individual contacts, tutors will often accompany their students to the community venue and oversee their work. This is possibly the simplest place to start as it remains largely within a tutor's control and can be carried out with the resource allocated to module teaching.	Where students from a single module identify their own projects or the university brokers a range of different projects for students to choose from. It is rarely possible for a university to provide the capacity to visit or support students on their projects and systems are needed for co-ordinating and communicating with partners and bringing students into university for support. Additional documentation, such as handbooks for students and partners, risk-assessment and sign-off sheets need to be planned in advance.

Larger pro-gramme	Where students from a course or department undertake a range of group projects, each supported by a module tutor. This programme would need some co-ordination and more consideration as to how the different projects link and how the university is presented to, and perceived by, different elements of the community.	Where students from a range of different courses all undertake individual projects. A proper brokering system is probably needed in order to communicate the offer to local groups and gather them together in one place to meet students. Such a programme is administratively heavy and would benefit from the additional support of a volunteering or placements office to ensure a comprehensive offer is presented to community organisations.
Faculty- or university-wide pro-grammes	A faculty-wide or university-wide programme is likely to involve a range of group or individual projects with different course leaders responding in different ways. It may include generic, cross-university modules as well as discipline-specific or bespoke modules. The programme would benefit from a clear engagement strategy and policies to protect students and partners. It is an opportunity for the learning from different programmes to be shared across departments and resources to be pooled. It would inevitably involve additional core funding to broker a broad range of community projects and support the development of new engaged modules.	

Where a programme or project starts will be determined by intentions, context and the money and capacity within an institution to support it. A programme might begin as a top-down university initiative to expand third-stream work, a request from community partners for student involvement in a particular project or the need of a course leader to enhance student learning.

While many universities in the UK and throughout Europe are catching up with US initiatives for engaged learning, their motives for engagement vary. Watson suggests that 'no self-respecting university or college would dare to lack a civic and community mission' (Watson, 2007) and most universities recognise the need to provide students with more than academic qualifications within their degree if they are to attract students in a competitive HE market. However the positioning of engagement in university mission statements and whether SCE is expected to deliver skills for citizenship or skills for employability can impact on the shape and ethos of the programme. While all universities are expected to give some consideration to third-stream work, some interpret this more in relation to business and economic engagement rather than community involvement. Consequently the term 'engagement' can mean different things in different contexts and mission statements use a variety of terms, each of which could suggest a different focus.

How the scope and intentions of a programme fit within the broader mission of a university will help determine the range of projects offered to students and the way they are encouraged to approach them, but it is not unusual to find in any one institution a range of social and economic priorities. As indicated in the table above these could be driven by:

- the university (as a top-down institutional initiative);
- the faculty (as a discipline-related initiative); and
- the community (as a request coming directly from a potential partner).

However, most projects, in order to get started, need a passionate and motivated individual prepared to think outside of the structures related to any one of these areas.

The examples below, taken from SCE projects in Brighton, illustrate each of these different initiatives and the role of individuals in taking them forward.

1. *A larger programme working with individual projects.* The first generic SCE module at the University of Brighton, 'Community and Personal Development', was set up in response to a mentoring programme, attempting to recruit and maintain students as mentors in a widening participation initiative. The institution had agreed to participate in a national programme which placed undergraduates in schools to mentor young people with no prior family experience of university. Finding

appropriate mentors and supporting them to do this was proving difficult, and there were insufficient funds in the programme budget to pay more than students could earn in casual labour. It was also important to gain commitment from student mentors and to avoid the role being seen as casual work. The person running the programme felt that linking the activities to a university module could mean students from different subject areas would be able to take it as an option within their courses. They would then be able to use taught curricula time to develop themselves as mentors and to reflect on the value of the relationship. The work needed for this would be part of, rather than in competition with, assessment pressures. The module was validated shortly after the 'Active' volunteering programmes were launched nationally and planned in collaboration with the Brighton Active scheme. Students were given the option of taking it to accredit a range of volunteering activities. It began the first year as an additional module or 'extra credits' but was incorporated into course programmes as course leaders began to see its value as part of a student's personal development. It started with six students the first year, 20 in the second and 200 in the third. Although it was started in response to a particular institutional initiative it gradually grew to incorporate a range of different student projects reflecting the priorities of different discipline areas.

2. *A single module, working with a group project* and set up by a lecturer in literature who was approached by a teacher at her children's school to ask whether she, and her students, might be interested in introducing Shakespeare to primary school pupils. Seeing this as a challenge, she incorporated discussions on story, the universality of story and adapting Shakespeare for children into her lectures. A number of her students were keen to work with the school and the lecturer identified a generic student engagement module to use as a framework through which she could validate a group drama project. She adapted the module developed for mentors using similar course material (on schools, curricula, how children learn) and the same reflective assessment tasks, but replaced the mentoring elements with an after-school drama project in which all her group participated. Students took on different roles in adapting text, supporting children and running workshops. They learned a lot about their ability to work with children and to bring literature alive. Inspired by the success of this module, her colleagues took on the same module framework and identified community-based projects in creative writing

95

and film-making. The eventually adapted the generic SCE module to validate a bespoke version suitable for their own school.

3. *A non-accredited experience working with a group project.* 'Active Pharmacy' is a project which evolved from an earlier project 'Dispensing with the Mystery', which was set up jointly by a pharmacy lecturer working with Active Student, the Brighton volunteering service, and which ran in 2006. It brings undergraduate pharmacy students and medication users together to enable both groups to learn from and to teach each other. After recruitment via the University of Brighton 'Active Student' programme, students volunteer to attend meetings at which medication users (usually older people's groups) are gathered. Once there, individuals or pairs of students will spend time with one of the older participants. The conversation is free to run its course but is centred on a two-way exchange of information. Students learn from the older person what the effect of having to take medication can be on a person's life. In addition, the older participant is able to ask questions about their medication. In most cases these questions can be answered by the student; however, in case of difficulty there is always a registered pharmacist in attendance to whom the student may refer. This project has not been fully integrated into the curriculum as to do so would compromise the two-way nature of the learning experience. Students would, necessarily, be more focused on what they needed from the session than on developing a shared experience.

Reading across these examples, we recommend two key principles to keep in mind. The first is start small. Whatever the driver for a new programme, starting small provides useful lessons that can be in-corporated into the design and development of future programmes. This learning can then be used to develop more successful larger pro-grammes once community contacts have been formed. Starting small also provides time for a programme to evolve in a way that is responsive to the local context and best meets the needs of students and partners. The second principle is to ensure a good fit. Whether started in response to an institutional priority, a faculty interest or a community request, it is important to be clear how any initiative fits with the priorities of discipline, the intentions of the university and the broader community context.

Locating SCE within the structure of the university

The operational issues

Many SCE projects take place under the radar as the result of personal contacts between an academic and a local community group, with lecturers bringing in 'real examples' as case studies for students to work on. Other community requests originate as volunteering opportunities and find their way to the discipline area most likely to take them on. However, if a university makes a strategic commitment to prioritising engagement work then a cross-institutional or community-facing unit makes interaction with external organisations easier.

People outside of a university tend to see any contact they have with students as representing 'the university' and tend not to differentiate between one course and another or even one university and another within the same town. Many cities house more than one university and understanding who comes from where and the different regulations and procedures of separate institutions can be confusing to community partners. Maintaining an awareness of the processes of a neighbouring university can make discussions with partners easier. The constraints and the challenges of working with one group of students can easily be transferred to the next with negative impacts as 'engagement' begins to happen on a larger scale. In some instances neighbouring institutions have experimented with sharing a database of student opportunities, or working together to provide a united response to emerging local issues.

The time and support needed to identify relevant projects and the confusion that can result from different parts of the university responding in different ways suggests that negotiating relationships with partners should form part of a broader customer relationship management (CRM) system. But the language and structure of CRMs, designed for business relationships with larger and well-organised institutions, can be intimidating to small community organisations which don't really fit within their categories and criteria. Central or cross-university 'support' departments don't often possess the infrastructure to manage an academic programme, to validate modules or to run exam boards and the credit-awarding elements of engagement will always need to be located within an academic school. However, the community-facing elements of engagement are often similar between different schools and disciplines and can benefit from being centrally located and shared. Universities have opted for different solutions in dealing with this, some combining social and economic engagement in a course or discipline related 'placements office', others working with a volunteering programme to source both accredited and non-accredited student opportunities. Although dealing with validation and assessment can happen in isolation from each other, there are many opportunities for joint learning between discipline areas and community projects rarely fit neatly within a single discipline.

The location of a university, whether campus or city based will also affect the ease with which partners come into the institution as well as students' ability to travel to local projects. Lessening the barriers between the two, by encouraging students to attend community events and bringing partners into the institution will help to ease communications and increase understanding of the priorities of different partners. Holding 'matching events' where different organisations come into the university to present projects to students, inviting partners to deliver taught elements of a course, or inviting partners to attend student presentations at the end of their course can all help to strengthen the relationships between partners and their understanding of each other's practice. Ultimately this makes the different elements of a course more cohesive and helps build stronger partnerships.

The academic issues

Generic cross-university engagement modules or those involving students from more than one discipline will still need to be located and administered by one school. There are arguments for and against creating a cross-university module with a range of generic learning outcomes and assessment tasks that can be adapted to different contexts. Students working on practical projects can gain a lot from being taught alongside those bringing different skills from another discipline and from sharing elements of a bigger community based task. It can be easier to 'try out' engagement in a new school by adapting a module that is already in existence and working within the structures put in place to support it. A generic module at Brighton was located initially in the School of Education then moved to the School of Social Sciences and run in Humanities, Environment and Technology, Business and Geography. But the learning outcomes have been criticised for being inaccessible to students without a social science background and the assessment tasks insufficiently visual for students whose major discipline is, for example, product design. The idea of cross-disciplinary working is often more attractive to academics than to students who prefer the safety of a known group with familiar language and conventions. Working outside of the university with community partners is in itself challenging without the further requirement of cross-disciplinary teams. The generic module in CUPP, after operating for ten years across seven different disciplines, is now in the process of being devolved to individual schools and adapted for their particular use. The intention is to manage external relationships centrally but to encourage individual schools to take ownership of the academic elements and to ensure SCE is linked more closely with other course modules. SCE can provide the opportunity to link theoretical perspectives discussed in a lecture with the use of these in a real-world context and this is more easily exploited when those delivering SCE modules are connected to the broader course programme in which it is located. One of the areas students struggle with most on engaged modules is the ability to process and to use theory, often seeing theory as something that should be 'shoehorned' into a particular assignment rather than informing and being informed by practice. The more that other course team members are able to relate their own teaching to the things that students are witnessing in the world, the more holistic the course and the experience.

Local priorities and the organisation of the not–for–profit sector

Having a sense of the key issues and key players in an area, and the tensions between them, is useful in identifying appropriate partners to work with. While a project may be constructed in response to a request from a particular group, having a sense of other actors, their values and policies and the contribution they make towards an area of work helps lecturers to contextualise projects and students to understand the range of responses to a local issue. Most cities have a local Council for Voluntary Services (CVS) or co-ordinating body that will have an overview of the different organisations in a locality and provide a training or a brokerage role, and they may be a useful long-term contact for the university helping connect individual project ideas with relevant partners.

This is also a good starting point for understanding the range of community and voluntary groups in an area and how they relate to statutory services. The sector will have its own histories and cultures of working, and by aligning itself with one organisation rather than another, a university can appear to override decisions made at local level.

The austerity measures of the years following 2008 have caused the demise and/or disappearance of a number of important organisations and left others vulnerable. Students will need to understand how services are funded, how funding policies affect provision and the political and policy imperatives behind them. A better understanding of the sector could, for example, result in a student project to support a temporary gap in provision and help to explain a confused or complex picture.

> **Example:** A group of lecturers in the business school had some indication of the difficulty experienced by local social enterprises, to market themselves effectively. They also recognised the potential for business students to take on individual marketing projects for community groups. Working with their local CVS they advertised the opportunity to work with a marketing student to a range of groups in the area. The CVS played a brokering role in inviting in different organisations to meet with students and providing some input into the marketing course on the differing priorities of voluntary and private sector organisations.

Gaining an understanding of local council priorities, an oversight of their development plans and the local strategic partners that exist in an area can also provide broader indications of the role that a university can usefully play in local issues. Such priorities might include, for example, the development of affordable housing, flood management, sustainable energy or community cohesion, each of which offers significant opportunities for meaningful student involvement. Gaining membership of city-wide boards (development partnerships or learning groups) requires an investment of time and energy but provides important contacts for collaborative work. It helps to ensure the university has a voice in strategic developments and represents itself as an equal partner in trying to address them.

Community representatives can also provide a valuable role in planning an engagement programme, inputting into taught elements, keeping the university up to date with policy changes and recommending areas for research. Forming long-term relationships with a few key local players can help to ensure that a student programme remains relevant to the community during the life of a programme that it has been set up to work with.

> **Example:** Membership of the Local Strategic Partnership (LSP) in Brighton drew attention to a bid they were developing for biosphere status in the area. Undergraduates from an environmental science programme got involved in the consultation process, inputting data from survey responses and helping to publicise the application. Other students from a postgraduate module took on analysis of the survey as part of a social research practice module and one of these provided some input into the final report as part of his dissertation. The raising of the issue within the LSP provided the initiative for a range of student projects at different levels and gave the university a proper role in the eventual biosphere bid.

Where does it fit in the curriculum?

Optional or core?

Most students come to university aware that gaining experience is important to their future, but some are also motivated by aspirations to make a difference in the world. However, while it may be attractive to institutions to establish an engaged module that all students undertake, experience has shown that making it compulsory for students to do community-based work is neither useful for them or for the organisations they work for. There is a danger that applied modules are seen either as work experience, sometimes repeating a course requirement that students undertook in secondary-level schooling, or as enforced voluntarism, where students are being made to volunteer. Placing a reluctant student into a busy community organisation can drain time and capacity from staff in trying to motivate them against their will and reflect badly on the university.

Students with external commitments on their time, particularly those with children, often struggle with the additional requirements that committing to an external organisation brings. While these may be equal in hours to the requirements of course study the arrangement of them is often less flexible. These hours often have to be scheduled to fit in with the daytime working hours of a community group and may not fit into either late-night or home-based study habits that can be used for desk-based work. It is easier to discuss values, notions of citizenship, rights and responsibilities, emotional literacy and personal development with a group who have opted to do this and shown an interest in it, than making it compulsory for a full course cohort. Identifying the range of opportunities available for those who want to do them and looking for ways in which students can contribute to a community organisation without always being there can open up possibilities for those who have strict demands on their time. These might include doing research for

---

Example: The new undergraduate programme designed for a recently opened campus of the University of Brighton had a generic community module at level 5 as core to all its programmes. Students complained bitterly about this at the end of the first year. A high proportion of mature students, many whom had worked for or been associated with voluntary groups in the town previously, objected to being told to work for them again as part of their studies. Many saw joining university as a way out of low-paid work with not-for-profit organisations and had aspirations to academic careers. This was resolved by adding a theoretical research element as an option for a project within the generic module. It meant minimal revalidation and enabled students who had family responsibilities to do this part of their project work from home after an initial consultation with an external group. The revised context description and assessment tasks are shown below.

This module will be undertaken in relation to one of the following contexts:

Work for the benefit of a particular community, organisation or institution in a voluntary or paid capacity:
- Part-time paid work for a local employer with some element of additional responsibility.
- Planned practical experience in a specific context relating to an area of possible future work
- A piece of paid or unpaid research or consultancy work

Projects can be identified within or outside the university and, subject to approval, undertaken individually or as part of a group.

Students will be required to complete the following tasks:

---

or preparing material to be used by a community group rather than attending to support a face-to-face session, but still help students to see the relevance of discipline study to real-world problems. Other examples have included compiling a literature review, analysing data, designing paper-based or electronic resources or taking on a consultancy role. If a course leader decides to make engagement a core element in a course it is important to ensure there are desk-based opportunities to work with communities for those who find themselves unable or unwilling to be directly involved.

Task 1 (weighting 50%)
Detailed analysis of the organisation – to include internal structures, mission statement, health and safety issues, lines of responsibility, a review of the culture and a critique of the organisation's effectiveness in the form of a report. Maximum 1500 words. (Learning objectives: 1, 2, 5)
OR
A research or consultancy report in response to a negotiated brief. The report should include an analysis of how the research fits within the organisations aims, mission statement and organisational culture. (Learning objectives: 1, 2, 5)

Task 2 (weighting 50%)
Reflective evaluation of interpersonal and organisational skills, with evidence, to include an outline of one situation that went badly and one that went well and a personal assessment, with examples, of time-keeping, ability to meet deadlines, ability to prioritise, to take responsibility and to work as part of a team, to include a structured learning log for the duration of the practical period. (Learning objectives: 3, 4, 6)

First, second, third year or postgraduate options

Deciding when and where to incorporate engagement into a student programme depends on the knowledge-base and the maturity needed to carry it out and the learning objectives set for the experience. Generally, the first semester of the first term is too soon and the final semester of the final term too late. On first arriving at university, new students have too much to cope with getting to know the environment and the institution to take on the additional requirements of a community organisation, although contact with the local community can be a valuable part of an induction process.

Examples

A politics programme asked students to visit and to hold discussions with a civil society organisation in the town as part of a first semester activity on 'What is politics and politics in the locality'. The meetings, attended in groups, helped to orientate them in the city and open up their views of what their course and their discipline might involve.

A freshers' programme included information on the community engagement strategy of the university and encouraged all new students to attend a 'make a difference day' in order to give a day of their time to a new volunteering project held six weeks into the first term.

A social event, called 'Another side of the city' brought in representatives from different minority groups within the town to meet with and talk to groups of students and share first hand other experiences of living in the city. Acting like resources in a 'living library' they were able to answer students' questions about some of the things they had encountered since arriving in a new place.

Establishing an awareness of both the engaged role of a university and the scope of any study programme can provide a valuable preparation for a deeper-engaged experience. However, the majority of experiential projects tend to be located in the second year of a study programme at a point when students are more secure in their environment and ready to be challenged in terms of their disciplinary learning.

An additional opportunity in the third or final year of a programme can build on some of the contacts and understanding developed during the middle year. Final-year students are often able to offer research skills or take on additional responsibility within an organisation. It might also be an opportunity to support or mentor new students or school leavers considering university. Supporting or facilitating the learning of others is often key to clarifying a student's own understanding of an issue and can be a valuable role for someone approaching final year assessments.

The range and focus of appropriate projects depends on course priorities and learning objectives, the interests and aspirations of the students involved and the needs of a community organisation. Ultimately there needs to be a balance between the priorities of students and those of the organisation with some negotiation between these if both sets of expectations are to be met. SCE tends to be more concerned with broadening a student's view of the world than linking them to a job they may do in the future so the scope for projects that meet the needs of community partners is potentially broader than in the case of work placements. A dental student, for example, was encouraged to take a project in a children's centre to develop his ability to relate to children and to reassure them when they were scared. A criminology student supported a youth centre to get to understand the pressures on young people that might cause them to offend. A community nursing student worked for a Roma support group in order to develop relationships with a group who rarely used local health facilities.

Postgraduate students are more likely to take on research projects with or for local community groups either as part of a research practice module or their final dissertation. More on student–community research can be found in Chapter 7.

Finding appropriate partners

Setting up and managing an engaged module takes time, but it also eventually provides learning hours that are spent away from the university. While much of the work is front-loaded, needing to happen prior to starting and in the early weeks of a course, essentially the module should be deliverable within course-related teaching hours, preparing all supporting materials for students in advance, holding extensive discussions with community partners and carrying out any risk assessment well before the module begins. The inclusion of group tutorials, action learning sets (see below) and intermittent seminars can provide appropriate support for a group of 15–20 students without demanding too many more hours from a lecturer than would be spent delivering any university programme. But small class sizes and low ratios between tutor and student are essential in order to develop personal relationships. Keeping students safe while challenging them to go beyond their comfort zone cannot happen without getting to know them as individuals.

If there is an intention to set up a larger, cross-university programme, as indicated in the earlier table in this chapter, then additional administrative hours are crucial to provide the documentation needed by students and partners and to properly broker projects. These could be identified by:

- working with a volunteering scheme which is already set up to liaise with community partners and assess the risks associated with projects. The volunteering office may be able to offer this facility to a credit-bearing programme, either by identifying relevant group projects or encouraging partner organisations to accept individual students looking for specific projects. Despite existing as an independent unit with its own contacts with voluntary sector organisations, CUPP continues to work with Active Student to find course-related student opportunities.
- working with a placements office, using their resources to contact and to log enquiries from community organisations or advise individual students. Placement offices, usually located in individual schools or departments, will have a reasonable knowledge of the students they are working with but often have an employability rather than a social engagement focus, and hence may have a more narrow interpretation of student opportunities.
- centralising the need for support in one administrative role which works across the university. This provides the opportunity to develop strong relationships with voluntary sector organisations and can broker project ideas between different organisations or across different departments, it can also often help bring students with different orientations and interests to work on a project together. CUPP will often use its own networks to advertise for specific opportunities to organisations in response to a new course related project, such as the chance to make a documentary film with a student group or devise a new business plan.

Examples

In Brighton we hold an annual 'matching event' in which community organisations are invited into the university to share information about their work and the contributions students might make towards it. Organisations are invited to submit a short brief about the role

106

which is circulated in advance to a student group. The event takes the form of a fair, with stalls on which organisations can create a display of their work. Students are invited into the fair throughout the afternoon, hunting down those opportunities they feel best meet with their own interests and having initial discussions with personnel on the stall. They can have an informal interview there and then and arrange a follow-up one at a later date.

While SCE programmes prioritise not-for-profit organisations, these include statutory service providers, national charities with local offices, civil society groups and social enterprises, and small community-based organisations. Some programmes also respond to requests from individuals or families who need support for a particular family member. Students have been asked, for example, to support children who are out of school for long periods or to act as social mentors for autistic young people who need support in building relationships.

While large, well-resourced organisations (schools, colleges and council offices) often have the capacity to absorb a number of students and see it as part of their mission to do so, negotiating and supporting successful student projects still takes time. If the organisation is too small or the family is acting alone there is a danger that either the student will receive inadequate support or the organisation will be required to give more than they gain. Acting as a responsible host places a number of demands on any voluntary organisation and there is always a danger of these outweighing the input they get in return. The most successful relationships tend to be those built on existing contacts, where one group has an understanding of the other, which is an additional argument for starting a programme with small numbers and building these up over time. Community groups can have unreasonable expectations about what a university can offer to a town and what an undergraduate student might be able to achieve. It is important to manage expectations. For example, community groups may be seeking free labour to carry out a range of relatively mundane tasks or easy access to skilled researchers or practitioners, neither of which is particularly helpful to creating a realistic and mutually beneficial programme. While many student projects have achieved a great deal, this has usually been where the relationship between both partners was strong and there was an equal commitment to its success.

The benefits for partners

Stoecker (Stoecker and Tyron, 2009) in his book *The Unheard Voices* draws attention to the very different needs and perspectives of community partners and the often unequal relationships between faculty and community when setting up student projects in the USA. He refers to the mix as a 'complex 3D jigsaw puzzle', and the mismatch between the attitudes of students, often significantly privileged in being able to attend HE in the first place, and the disadvantaged young people who live in the neighbourhoods in which they may go to work. He questions whether engagement programmes are in danger of exacerbating inequality rather than addressing it.

Stoecker also draws attention to the attitude of faculty towards engagement, how community partners tend to be ready to see themselves as learners, keen to learn alongside the students they accept, while faculty can position themselves as experts, primarily concerned with either their own research or the learning of their students. To collaborate effectively with community partners it is important to value the knowledge they bring, alongside and equal to the knowledge of academics. Added to this, students, if not prepared properly, will be overly focused on 'getting their project done, their assessment finished, processing the new experiences they are encountering' rather than providing something of value to the community. He discusses the motives of community organisations in engaging with universities and identifies four main themes which are not dissimilar to the kind of responses we have had from partners in the UK:

- Organisations see it as part of their mission to educate others about the issues they deal with
- Organisations hope to build their own capacity by working with students who bring particular skills
- Organisations depend on volunteers and students offer free and often energetic labour
- Organisations are keen to develop long-term connections with university

None of these positions need to be incompatible with a university or a student agenda. Taking time to understand the needs and expectations of partners at the start of any project and explaining the limitations of a university to respond, give the relationship a better chance of succeeding.

Partners may not, for example, realise the time-bound nature of student involvement, the restrictions of semester timetables and the short period of the year in which students are available. Encouraging long-term partners to have projects ready to fit in with the academic year (in the UK generally an October start and a May finish) and to be aware of possible student intakes and assessment deadlines can enable them to develop relevant student projects that are also manageable.

The use of language and perceptions of unequal power relationships can also create a barrier to good joint working. Community groups can feel intimidated by the size and resources of a university and the status often given to academics. Both universities and community organisations use large amounts of jargon and acronyms, often thoughtlessly, that need explaining to the outside world. The relative availability of resources in a university, administrative staff, photocopying facilities, funded phone calls, and travel expenses are often unavailable within a community group with limited funding. Asking for forms to be filled in, procedures circulated or visits to be made to the university can all come at a personal cost to a community worker with no budget. The time needed to negotiate a project and to support students who are new to community-based work can also put pressure on a small organisation with limited resources if they don't then receive substantial student input in return. For projects to make a worthwhile contribution at community level they will need sufficient time for students to move beyond their own orientation period to become effective workers. It can often be a significant time period before a student moves from being a net cost to making a net contribution.

Some programmes encourage students to find their own opportunities and to approach either personal contacts or volunteering agencies to identify a project that links with their studies. While organisations generally have their own processes for interviewing and dealing with volunteers, a credit-bearing programme puts additional pressures on the capacity of an organisation and carries additional risks. While volunteers are often motivated by the work of the organisation and their own wish to give something back to them, students have an additional focus on their assessment and a timetable associated with this. The learning that students are required to do might mean they reflect on their project role work and add an additional, considered perspective, but they bring an anxiety about 'getting their required hours completed' and the possibility that they may suddenly leave when this has been done. If students are asked to identify their own projects some kind of contract pro forma, to be shared with the organisation, would enable them to be upfront about their own requirements.

Planning for risk

Keeping people safe, both students themselves and those they are working with, is paramount in work of this nature. Sending students to work in difficult or challenging circumstances always carries an element of risk, but these can be anticipated, and mitigated in different ways.

Different institutions have their own risk-assessment strategies and policies, and a new programme needs to move carefully between over-protection with policies that are sufficiently risk averse to prevent any activity, and recklessness. If students are to work with young or vulnerable people in any face-to-face contact they will need to undertake a series of legal checks. Keeping up to date with the changing requirements, the costs and the timescale associated with these is important as they can negatively impact on the time needed for students to arrange and agree their projects.

Organisations working with vulnerable groups will probably have their own systems for carrying out necessary checks with new personnel and inducting staff, but without a clear timetable for this there is a danger that projects will not be realisable within the timeframe set for the module. With projects involving vulnerable groups it could be important to deal with risk and insurance issues in the term before the module is due to start (Chapter 7 of this book deals with what can go wrong in more depth). Until recently the government system of CRB checks was designed to ensure service users were safe from volunteers and workers and required an extensive 'criminal records bureau check' on all new workers. This was expensive and time consuming for organisations and, while based on an important initiative, often debarred students from getting involved in projects because of the time taken in getting clearance to do so. The revision of this into a simpler DBS system (Disclosure and Barring Service) came into place in 2012. This new system allows people working with vulnerable groups to apply for a check online themselves, which will be sent straight to their employer. They are able to use their former checks with new employers as this will automatically be updated with any new convictions.

Keeping students involved with the deeper elements of their learning, particularly in periods when they are meeting less often for seminars, is important. If a project doesn't start on time, a student can become overwhelmed or demotivated and there are invariably implications for end-of-year assessments and exam boards. Finding out that a project has gone wrong at the end of the year makes it more difficult to rectify. Regular check-in or hand-in points, when groups submit their learning contracts or first reports, periodic submission of blogs, meeting for group tutorials and so on, can all provide early warning signs of projects going wrong.

Keeping partners involved and making sure they are getting what they want is also preferable to finding out from an end-of-year evaluation that the student was unreliable or the project failed. But regular visits to community organisations hosting students are generally not possible in large-scale modules with different community organisations. Providing partners with a handbook outlining course procedures, what they might expect from students, and a named contact within the institution can help, and are more likely to be used when a good relationship with the organisation has been established. Building up good relationships with partners over time, continuing to network and encouraging partners onto campus wherever possible helps to keep dialogues alive and open (see the section 'Risk-assessment, insurance and ethical procedures for SCR' in Chapter Seven).

References

Gelmon, S.B., Holland, B.A., Seifer, S.D., Shinnamon, A.F. and Connors, K. (1998) 'Community-university partnerships for mutual learning', *Michigan Journal of Community Service Learning*, 5, pp. 97–107.

Stoecker, R. and Tyron, E. with Holgendorf, A. (2009) *The Unheard Voices Community Organizations and Service Learning*. Philadelphia, PA: Temple University Press.

Watson, D. (2007) *Managing Civic and Community Engagement*. Milton Keynes: Open University Press.

CHAPTER SIX

Developing student–community engagement

Introduction

The chapter looks in more depth at the range of projects in an SCE programme and the things to consider when working with community partners. It includes sections on individual and group projects, those initiated by students, faculty or community and on module design. It discusses the significance of community-based research and looks at Student Community Research (SCR), where students take on research on behalf of their communities, as an element of SCE. It suggests some resources for supporting reflective learning and offers exemplars for module aims and objectives and learning contracts.

What kind of projects work well?

The kinds of project that fit best with an engaged learning programme will depend on the priorities set for the module and the ethos behind a university's strategy. Marullo and Edwards (2000) discuss the difference between student-initiated projects (where students design a project and feel ownership of it) faculty-initiated projects (where faculty design and initiate a project and students participate, often as part of a group) and community-initiated projects (where students respond to a project brief designed by the community and fulfil an existing role (Marullo, 2000). Their discussion draws from Boyer's work in outlining the scholarship of discovery, based in a purely scientific paradigm, which tends to dominate in HE in the USA, and a scholarship of engagement which encompasses discovery, pedagogy, integration and application (Boyer, 1990). It also reflects some of the difference between a science shop approach –

which in the Netherlands tends to broker scientific questions emerging from local community, and some of the Canadian work on community-based research. In the former, students, working mainly from a scientific paradigm, answer questions for communities. In the latter, students work with communities to identify a project, frame questions to be answered or problems to be solved, work together on resolving these and place a high value on the co-creation of knowledge.

In Brighton we have worked with projects framed in very different ways:

Student designed:

- Students have worked in groups to analyse a particular community or neighbourhood, facilitate discussions with local people around problems areas or issues they are most concerned about, and work with them to try to identify solutions, pooling students' scientific knowledge with the contextual knowledge of neighbourhood residents. The students brought skills of research design and analysis, and locals brought a greater understanding of what it means to live in an area and what solutions might work. Postgraduate students trained as community organisers have tended to favour projects developed in this way as they are skilled in participatory approaches and have the community contacts to develop a viable project with local groups. Examples have included working with a group of young people to design a skate park or to launch a community café.
- Individual students have project ideas, based their own passionate concerns, and generally connected to a community of interest. They have used the university's network of local organisations to find an organisation willing to host their project and work with them to make it a reality. Postgraduate dissertation students often work in this way as it enables them to choose their own research topic, to gain access to a research field, to work scientifically and independently, and to apply their results. Examples have included identifying the impact of government austerity measures on families on benefit or

the value of sensory play to severely disabled children, and as postgraduates they welcomed the freedom to negotiate their own briefs with partners.

- Students from a politics programme worked with those from an Environment and Media course to identify a particular issue they cared about and to launch a campaign in response to it. They were encouraged to use their individual skills of social movements, environmental science and the use of media to identify a group to work with and to design, run and evaluate a campaign about an issue of their choice. This required skills in group work, local analysis, interdisciplinary working, planning and design which on an undergraduate programme proved a challenge. Examples included a radio campaign to increase membership of Greenpeace and a multimedia campaign to address recycling on campus buildings. While the option sounded exciting at the outset, some groups struggled to work across disciplines and with the amount of freedom the brief gave them. Many asked for more structure and guidance on what they should focus on and needed the support of an organisation to help shape their plans.

Faculty designed:

- A lecturer working with a disabled arts group realised the potential for arts students to benefit from the work of disabled artists while, in turn, supporting those artists in developing their art making. She designed an undergraduate module called 'Access to Art' in which visual art students worked one to one with a disabled artist on collaborative projects. While it took some time to set up the project and agree arrangements for the disabled arts group to come into the university it has since run for many years. Art students who have signed up for this module have commented on how much they have learned about art making from their partner and how their own drawing has been freed up as a result. The disabled artists have now formed their own company selling their work

114

and the lecturer has gone on to develop a full MA using a similar approach.

- Community Media 4 Kenya (CM4K) is a community media partnership run by Dr Peter Day from the School of Art, Design & Media that draws on experiential learning processes of a final-year undergraduate BA (Hons) Media Studies module (LM376 Community Project). LM376 was first run ten years ago as a CUPP-sponsored module and focused on community media partnerships in Brighton and Hove. In recent years, the focus has shifted to partnerships in Kenya but the module's rationale has remained constant. CM4K's community-based learning approach seeks to enrich student learning through dialogic community engagement, while strengthening and empowering communities in sustainable ways through community media projects that meet the needs of participating community partners. CM4K has been developing a 'participatory educational and action learning scenarios' (PEARLS) approach to community-based learning. The PEARLS approach requires students to engage, through dialogic action, with partners to map assets and identify needs; assess how assets might be used to address needs; plan and develop all aspects of the partnership activities; create and test the interventions in the field; and reflect critically with partners dialogically at each stage of the process. To date, much of the CM4K work has focused on student facilitation of capacity-building workshops with community partners through a 'training the trainers' approach.

Community designed:

- A local voluntary organisation provides mentoring support to pre- and post-release prisoners, many of whom are young men who repeatedly offend. They contacted the university about training students to act as mentors and regularly attract high levels of student interest, particularly from criminology students. They now design their training courses around students' availability. Their programme is tight but fits within a university module and undergraduates learn a lot from it about how the penal system works and what leads people to reoffend.

- The local police force contacted the university looking for a student to design a phone app that could support young men apprehended via 'stop and search' procedures. It linked them directly to a website outlining their rights and with guidance on how to respond to stop and search procedures. A computing student was able to respond to this as part of a postgraduate module and the police have since been able to publicise the app, which can now apparently be downloaded during a 'stop and search' procedure.

- A range of voluntary organisations contact the university every year with requests for research. These are logged in a database and made available to postgraduate students as they begin looking for dissertation topics. Students are supported in negotiating and agreeing the projects to ensure that the final outcome meets the expectations of both groups and can be achieved within a realistic timescale.

Table 6.1 summarises the advantages and challenges of these different kinds of projects.

Marullo and Edwards (2000) discuss the difference between charity or welfare projects as opposed to social justice or rights-based projects and the learning potential each might offer to students. They suggest that charity projects with a service delivery intention do little to challenge longer-term or structural inequalities. By framing social problems in terms of individual, immediate need, they fail to draw attention to the social context that lies behind this and broader issues of power or injustice. Stoecker (2003) categorises the different approaches taken by voluntary organisations and links these to a functionalist or a conflict model of society:

Table 6.1

Project type	Student designed	Faculty designed	Community designed
Character-istics	Project designed by an individual student or by a small group, based on an issue they care about and often then located with a community group.	Project designed to fit needs of a particular discipline or module, often in partnership with a community organisation.	A brief for a role or activity designed by a community group and advertised among a range of relevant students.
Advantages	Often deep commitment to a project, learning associated with project cycles, needs assessment, planning delivery, evaluation and budgeting.	Likely to have strong links between practical and theoretical elements, could be designed to incorporate whole group and to link smoothly between taught, face-to-face and community-based elements.	Generally based in the organisation and reflecting its mission and values, simulates the process of finding employment in application and interview, requires individual students to adapt to organisational cultures.
Dis-advantages	More suited to third years or postgraduates than first- or second-year students, higher risk of going wrong, not necessarily fully representative of community need or of discipline–related learning outcomes.	More oriented towards the needs of the institution and the course, less challenging to individual students who often have less opportunity to exercise their own initiative.	May be harder to make links between theory and practice or to fit into a university programme.
Example	School safety campaign, making a promotional video.	Drama workshop, mentoring programme.	Staffing an advice centre, setting up a database.

Table 6.2

Type of organisation	Conflict view of society	Functionalist view of society	Student roles
Agency	Organisation has an advocacy role, students can learn to represent.	Social service or social care, students learn to serve.	Students play a role in a larger organisation, confronted with structures and systems.
Grass roots	Community organising, students learn value of participation.	Community development, student involvement in capacity-building.	Students often involved in front-line work.
Dangers and challenges of the different models	Danger of challenging and undermining rather than working with existing structures.

View of community as oppressed and needing to overturn the status quo. | Danger of a welfare approach to inequality by focusing on the problem rather than the causes of the problem.

View of community as needing support to have their voices heard or to have things done for them. | |

(Adapted from Stoecker [2003])

Like Marullo and Edwards, Stoecker is concerned that partnerships with welfare or service delivery programmes, unlike advocacy programmes, fail to draw attention to or challenge the causes of social inequality. He suggests that universities placing students in welfare organisations should encourage them to analyse the deeper social context in which the organisation operates and the causes of social injustice. Discussions on ways of introducing these perspectives into module delivery are discussed further in Chapter Seven ('Drawing on mentors and alumni and establishing a community of practice').

While there are many successful service delivery projects that have a valuable impact on the local community, it is useful to develop an awareness of the power structures that underlie these and the value base of the organisations running them or providing project funds. SCE provides an opportunity for students to examine their own values and priorities to gain a deeper understanding of questions of equity and social justice. Providing the organisation offers proper induction and support, students have sufficient autonomy and responsibility to make a valuable contribution and the module encourages them to see their project in a broader cultural and policy context, there is learning to be gained from a broad range of project opportunities attached a wide range of disciplines. Examples in Brighton have included projects in architecture, the business school, humanities, education, pharmacy, arts, sports science, journalism, languages, geography, product design, sustainable technology, media and environment, broadcast media and life sciences as well as health and social sciences.

Establishing a learning contract

As in any partnership agreement, some kind of learning contract is important to establish the roles and responsibilities of the different partners carrying out the work. If a student is undertaking a practical role for a local organisation then an outline of the roles and responsibilities of each partner and the training or risk assessments needed might be sufficient. In a longer term, more complex project involving research or design, consideration should be given to the intellectual property rights of what is produced, how the product or outcomes will be used, when they will be ready and a communication strategy to cover meetings and exchange of information in the lead up to the final product. Real-world assignments are at risk of being delayed, changing direction or losing priority among a range of competing demands. If a project is to be completed in time for a student to graduate, having a clear project management and communications strategy can help to ensure both parties get what they need. In addition, student–community research (SCR) projects require careful negotiation with a partner to look at the different understandings and expectations of research and to agree a realistic timetable for completing it. This is crucial to it having a chance of being successful for both partners. (See also the later section, 'Communities and Research: SCR within SCE'.)

Two examples of learning agreements developed in Brighton have been included below. A final completed document is normally around 3–4 pages in length.

Example: Learning contracts, undergraduate

Name of student:

Module tutor:

Name of organisation:

Contact person within the organisation:
(Please include contact details)

A description of your task or role:

Dates and times you will be working:

A short explanation of why you have chosen this project and how it relates to your work:

Texts you will read to support your work (please give a couple of examples under each heading):

Policy and context:

Organisations:

Skills:

Please give a short summary on why you have chosen these texts and how they relate to your work *(up to 500 words)*

Any training, insurance or police checks needed (please describe what these are and how long they will take)

STUDENT COMMUNITY RESEARCH – AGREEMENT FORM

This agreement is between:

Student name:

Course:

Name of community contact:

Role:

Organisation:

It constitutes the research agreement and the schedule and responsibilities associated with this as well as the rights associated with the final product.

SCOPE OF PROJECT

The project consists of (please include aims, objectives, methods to be used in research):

RESOURCES ASSOCIATED WITH THIS PROJECT

In order to complete this project the following equipment and resources (e.g. expenses) are necessary.

Please specify any resources that are needed for completion of the project in terms of equipment or expenses and who will be responsible for supplying these.

TIME SCHEDULE AGREED FOR THIS PROJECT

In order to complete this project in a timely fashion we agree to work to the following milestones:

Date	Milestone	Person responsible	Notes/risks

COMMUNICATION STRATEGY FOR THIS PROJECT

In order to ensure the full involvement of all parties in this project we agree to communicate at the following intervals and in the following ways.

Please, state details of how and when you will communicate with each other, e.g.: weekly phone calls, monthly minuted meetings, etc. and any incidences where you cannot proceed without contacting the other e.g.: in agreeing to expenses etc.

It might be helpful to specify what needs to be communicated in writing, what is sufficient by email and when or how often you need to meet.

It might also be useful to indicate who to contact if one of the key specified contacts is not available.

RESPONSIBILITIES ASSOCIATED WITH THIS PROJECT

We both recognise the separate expertise of the different parties associated with this project. As such we have agreed the following areas of responsibility.

EXPECTED OUTPUTS FROM THIS PROJECT

We acknowledge here that different parties have different expectations from this project in terms of both experience and products. We have agreed to work together to try and produce the following.

Please indicate here the separate outputs each party expects from this project. This could include a research report, a full dissertation, a summary of outcomes, a presentation to the board of an organisation, learning around a particular area of the production of a piece of media or art work.

OWNERSHIP OF PRODUCTS ASSOCIATED WITH THIS PROJECT

We acknowledge that each party will have intellectual property rights associated with the following products and once this project has finished can use them as they wish. We expect the following acknowledgement as specified below:

You may wish to specify this in relation to the separate products of this project, e.g. the thesis, the research report or the DVD, etc. You might specify the conditions in which it can be use, any restrictions or requirements on the period of time in which it is viable or acknowledgements necessary.

Signed by

Student(s):

Organisation:

Name:

Date:

Adding practical experiences to existing modules or writing new ones?

Individual tutors interested in community engagement might start by adding an experiential project into an existing module, rather than go through the process of module revalidation. It is often possible to either adapt the content of a module without rewriting learning outcomes or add an extra-curricular experience to a module for students to draw on in their assignments. Module revalidation takes time and if an opportunity arises to get involved in some valuable hands-on work the best option may be to find creative ways to fit it into a current course structure.

> **Example**
>
> A lecturer in journalism ran a module in broadcast media that drew students from a range of humanities programmes. She initially co-taught the module with a BBC journalist and invited in a range of guest speakers, but was keen for her students to get a real understanding of the complexities of programme design. She made contact with a local radio station in the area that was willing to give small groups of students a radio slot to design, research, present a local news programme. They agreed on a whole-day project in which students visited the station and worked in small groups to identify and research news items, ready to present them in ten-minute slots. Working from local newspapers they identified stories they felt were newsworthy and tried to secure interviews with people involved. The activity was pressured and chaotic but left most students feeling proud of what they had achieved. However, when she repeated this the following year
>
> with a new group of students the stress levels seemed to outweigh the advantages and the majority of the group felt they had lost rather than gained in confidence from the experience. She used the experience to make contact with an alternative radio station and worked with them to jointly design an experience that would work for the station and the students.

Piloting a community project within an existing module can help to inform the design of new modules and ensure they properly take the needs of students and partners into account.

Important things to consider when writing new modules include:

- *Aims for the module and how far these reflect community as well as learning needs.* Do the aims involve learning for citizenship (promoting an understanding of rights and responsibilities), learning for employability (developing work-related skills and experience) or the application of theory to practice in order to enhance discipline-related knowledge? In each case, will the aims also make sense to a community organisation and provide them with what they need?
- *How the module will be assessed and who will do the assessing?* Will there be an assessment of the project experience and how well students worked within this? Will partners have a role in assessing students and how far can a piece

of practical work completed for a partner be built into
the final assessment tasks? *Embedding Public Engagement in
the Curriculum: A Framework for the Assessment of Student
Learning from Public Engagement* (Owen and Hill, 2011)
could be useful in considering the scope of both learning
outcomes and assessment tasks. It specifies the five areas for
assessment as: Co-creation of knowledge; management of
engagement; awareness of self and others; communication;
and reflective practice and provides guidelines on what to
look for when marking these different areas.

- *The balance of experiential and taught elements of the course and
  how these fit together.* Are taught elements front-loaded in
  order to prepare students for project work, bi-weekly in
  order to support project work as it develops or delivered
  in two halves framing a project period? Brighton has
  examples of all these models and each has advantages and
  disadvantages. Front-loading teaching and terminating
  seminars as projects begin leaves students without regular
  support when they are confronted with the challenges of
  community work. Bi-weekly slots create confusion for
  everyone and irregular attendance at community projects.
  Holding a series of initial seminars before a period of
  project work, with a further series to follow it, provides
  class-based support in finding and contextualising projects
  and again in preparing assessments but the two halves of a
  module can feel disjointed and leaves several weeks of no
  contact in between.

- *A fixed or fluid opportunity for experiential work.* Placement
  modules tend to identify particular days or weeks in
  which students are based outside the university. A group
  project may be able to happen in a similar way with
  defined times for project activity. However, in modules
  where students choose their own project opportunities
  a lot more flexibility is needed. Different roles will offer
  very different attendance patterns, from weekly meetings
  at a drop-in centre to a single intensive residential period
  on a holiday project or varied hours spent on a piece of
  consultancy work that a student might complete at home.
  While the number of project hours should be stipulated

these will be rolled out around fixed tutor-led sessions.

- *The range of contexts in which projects can be carried out.* A module descriptor will need to articulate the range of contexts in which projects can be located, whether in public, not-for-profit or private sectors, whether working for, or in partnership with, a particular organisation and whether it can include consultancy work done away from an organisation but using terms of reference set by them. It should include an awareness of the limitations some students may experience or the constraints on their time and mobility in order to ensure students have an equal opportunity to both identify projects and to make a meaningful contribution. This includes those students who for practical reasons are unable to attend an organisation during working hours, those who have difficulty in moving about the city or those whose aspirations are for self-employment in the future. Where modules have been made core within a course, having an independent piece of work as one of the options provides students with a greater degree of choice over where and how they work.

Example from a module descriptor:

Module context

This module will be undertaken in relation to one of the following contexts:

- Work for the benefit of a particular community, organisation or institution in a voluntary or paid capacity
- Part-time paid work for a local employer with some element of additional responsibility
- Planned practical experience in a specific context relating to an area of possible future work
- A piece of paid or unpaid research or consultancy work
- Projects can be identified within or outside the university and, subject to approval, undertaken individually or as part of a group

---

- *The number of hours given to a project-based experience and the need to ensure this is sufficient to be valuable to the student and the organisation.* While a module's learning hours are dictated by the credits awarded to it, face-to-face project

127

work needs time for relationships to develop and students need time to get to grips with the underlying issues in a complex organisation. A project lasting 20 hours can be too short to be meaningful or useful to either partner.

- *A one- or two-semester module.* The time taken to identify project opportunities, particularly where students are sourcing these themselves, can put undue pressure on a one-semester module. Where possible, a two-semester module provides a longer period in which to gain relevant project clearances and to develop relationships. In situations where this is not possible, allowing students to identify their projects in advance could enable them to begin to get projects underway.
- *Bespoke or generic learning outcomes.* If learning outcomes are written for a particular project they can be more specific in terms of content, learning and support materials. Generic modules, available for a range of different courses across an institution need to be sufficiently specific to be measurable, but broad enough to embrace a range of discipline areas. They may, for example, refer to the ability to apply theoretical perspectives to practical contexts, to understand policy initiatives and their significance to practice, to analyse the roles or structures of different organisations or to reflect on personal aspirations and achievements (see Owen and Hill, 2011).

Here are some examples of aims and learning outcomes for different level modules. Those at Levels 6 and 7 include a deeper level of analysis and more complex assimilated tasks.

Community Engagement Theory into Practice, Generic Module, Level 5

Module aims
- To provide a practical experience to help prepare for employment and to determine the areas and contacts on which you might focus
- To understand the relationship of theory into practice

- To gain a deeper understanding of organisations, how they work and where you might best fit within them
- To gain experience of dealing professionally with what may be challenging interpersonal situations and to explore a range of options for coping with these
- To develop an increased awareness of your personal skills and the importance of continuous learning and reflection
- To extend your awareness of the broader social, environmental and structural issues within the world in which you live

Learning outcomes

By the end of this module students will be able to:

1. Understand the concept of transferable skills and the need to adapt them to the requirements of context (outline plan)
2. Understand concepts of community and of personal development and ways of reviewing and extending interpersonal skills (reflective evaluation)
3. Understand the way organisations are structured and function and relate the structure and culture of the organisation in which they are placed to different theoretical models (organisational analysis)
4. Reflect on the relationship of theory to practice; apply theoretical concepts to real situations demonstrating the ability to prioritise, to meet deadlines, to act appropriately and to accept responsibility – either individually or as part of a team (reflective evaluation)
5. Formulate an outline of strengths, weaknesses and preferred working and learning styles in relation to possibilities in their future working lives (reflective evaluation)
6. Use clear presentation styles in written work, including grammar, spelling, layout and referencing in keeping with the university systems (organisational analysis)

Community Engagement Theory into Practice, Generic Module, Level 6

Module aims

- To provide an opportunity for a student to explore a complex work or consultancy context in which they use creativity and initiative to complete a specified project
- To explore the interplay of policy, theory and practice in a practical and discipline related context
- To develop confidence in the ability to make professional decisions based on evidence and to apply theory appropriately
- To make a valuable practical contribution to a not-for-profit organisation

Learning outcomes

By the end of the module students should be able to:

1. Complete an appropriate specified project within the time set and to the satisfaction of the organisation concerned
2. Critically analyse a series of key theoretical debates within the work context chosen
3. Understand the significance of policy initiatives to practical situations and articulate the impact of recent organisational and national policy developments within a specified context
4. Identify any individual contributions made to the completion of the task and the learning acquired as a result of these
5. Reflect critically on personal values, priorities and aspirations and justify a particular career pathway in the light of these

---

Community Engagement in Practice; Humanities Module, adapted from generic version, Level 6

Module aims

- Provide opportunities for students to explore and develop their knowledge and skills in a community or organisational context

- Enable students to use creativity, creative practice and initiative to complete a specific project

- Explore the interplay of policy, theory and practice in a practical context

- Develop students' confidence in the ability to apply their creative processes, vocational skills and academic knowledge in to a real-life context

- Give students opportunities to directly contribute to an organisation's, a project's or institution's remit

Learning outcomes

1. Complete an agreed and relevant project that fulfils a working brief

2. Give a critical account of a project or intervention incorporating relevant theoretical debates

3. Demonstrate knowledge of the significance of policy initiatives to practical situations and articulate the impact of recent organisational and local or national policy developments within a specified context

4. Identify specific contributions that their own creative and professional practices has had on the project

5. Critically reflect on their own vocational, personal and professional development derived from the project

---

Partnership and Participation with Marginalised Groups, Bespoke Nursing Module Level 6 and 7

Module aims

- To trace the history behind partnership working in the UK and its rationale
- To understand what constitutes marginalisation and who is marginalised in different contexts
- To work in partnership with voluntary organisations to address one particular issue and evaluate the approach used

Learning outcomes

1. Identify those groups and communities that are unable to access particular health and social care services and the reasons behind this

2. Critically analyse theoretical, ethical and practical aspects of networking and participation with marginalised groups

3. Critically analyse the significance of organisational culture and cultural beliefs and their effect on accessibility of health and social care services

4. Examine own beliefs and values in relation to definitions of health, social care and service provision, acknowledging the limitations of both personal and professional role

5. Utilise knowledge gained to design, implement and evaluate a practice intervention with an identified group to promote access to health and social care

6. Demonstrate a deeper understanding of the significance of partnership and participation in reaching marginalised communities

Developing reflective learning

Reflective learning is central to developing a student's understanding of themselves, the people they are working with and the context in which they are based. It is a core element of lifelong learning, and the basis for personal and professional development and has been seen as integral to any Service Learning or SCR programme. Dewey refers to reflection as 'a kind of thinking that consists of turning a subject over in the mind and giving it serious and consecutive consideration' (Dewey, 1933, p. 3), suggesting a logical approach and deductive reasoning. Schön (1987) is concerned with professional reflective practice and sees value in the uncertainties a new experience brings. Schön differentiates between reflection *in* action (thinking through the best course of action while involved in a new experience) and reflection *on* action (retrospectively thinking through the consequences of your actions and alternative possibilities). In the UK, Annette (2003) and O'Connor *et al.* (2011) talk about the importance of reflection in the UK in developing notions of democratic citizenship. Bourner (2013) sees the introduction of reflection into academia as a result of developments in the teaching of education or health professions as key to the success of SCE in academic circles. Jenny Moon's work is now used in a variety of formats within HE programmes to teach reflective approaches (1999, 2001, 2006).

Moon takes time to explain the different approaches to reflection and increased levels of reflexivity. Her work on learning journals and the handbooks she has produced for university students present reflection as:

> ... *a form of mental processing – like a form of thinking – that we use to fulfill a purpose or to achieve some anticipated outcome. It is applied to relatively complicated or unstructured ideas for which there is not an obvious solution and is largely based on the further processing of knowledge and understanding and possibly emotions that we already possess.* (Moon, 2001, p. 2)

Her paper on HE and learning (2001) takes readers through a range of approaches to reflective practice. These range from learning logs and learning journals to video diaries or peer discussion. She also draws attention to how some students struggle with this. The shift to writing in the first person and analysing experience and emotions as well as text and fact in an academic context seems to challenge all the dominant messages of secondary and higher education.

Experience of introducing reflective journals to students in Brighton over a number of years indicates how difficult it can also be to make these either meaningful or regular. Approaches have included online blogs shared among a group of students, a shared wiki in which students add to a group understanding of something based on their experience, structured logs requiring students to respond to particular questions are regular specified intervals, video diaries with oral reflections on a day's events and simple handwritten notebooks written on the bus on the way home. The range of reflective material produced as a result can vary from a minute-to-minute description with little deep understanding of it, to an outpouring of emotions and stream of consciousness writing that reflects strong feelings but makes little attempt to process them, to diaries written the night before an assignment hand in with added last-minute coffee stains to make them look as if they have been produced over the course of the module.

Guidelines on introducing reflective writing include:

- being clear about the purpose of reflection, the different meanings of reflection and what students should reflect on;
- emphasising the difference between reflective, critical and strategic thinking and the value of each for different purposes (see Chapter Four, section 'The importance of questioning');
- introducing students to reflective writing by asking them to describe an incident, analyse that incident and then reflect on that incident and to share their writing with each other highlighting the differences between the three approaches;
- illustrating the similarities to and differences from academic or diary writing, the importance of honesty and regularity in tracking a personal journey over time;
- giving students the choice of a range of formats, whether typed on a computer or written in a notebook, as a video diary for example, using whatever works for them;
- providing some examples of the work of other students and of the different levels of reflection for students to work through (including those in Moon [2004]);
- encouraging students to share learning from their reflections with each other in small groups at the start of a seminar;
- providing students with questions to guide their reflective thinking (as in Moon [2004] and in Chapter Four, section 'The importance of questioning')

A Freirean model of praxis; action, linked to reflection, leading to more informed action is relevant here (see Ison [2010] and Bunyan [2000]). There is further discussion on reflection in Chapters Five to Eight.

Communities and research: SCR within SCE

Community-engaged work is often linked to the principles of community-based or participatory action research. Some universities in the USA use the term course-based action research (CBAR) to encompass community-focused research, community-based experiential learning, and participatory action research. Their underlying principles include engaging undergraduates, faculty, and local partners in participatory work through a shared goal of improving the lives of members of marginalised communities, ... designing research in collaboration with local communities, ... connecting students with local level politics and deepening their concern for and participation in social justice (Hofmann, 2007).

The values underlying community-based research (CBR) and participatory action research (PAR) are relevant to much of the engagement work taking place in the UK. They include collective, self-reflective inquiry undertaken jointly by researchers and participants; their intention is to enable those involved in a situation to gain a deeper understanding of it and from this the ability to change it. Using a similar model of praxis, PAR uses reflection linked to action informed by an understanding of history, culture, and local context and embedded in social relationships.

Unlike traditional research, PAR does not aim to be either impartial or removed from those involved and the reflective cycle draws all participants into direct involvement in and reflection on each stage of the research process. An analysis of power relationships may be central to the research process, deliberately sharing power and shifting the boundaries between the objects and subjects of the research. It involves a shift, in that those who are researched become partners in the research process and have a voice in both what is investigated and how it is analysed and used (Baum et al., 2006). By bringing together academic and practitioner knowledge PAR draws attention to the different types of knowledge and their dual importance in gaining a holistic understanding of any context.

Understanding the values and the approach of PAR and CBR provides students with an important way in to understanding many of the key principles of engagement work. Questions about how knowledge is created and used alongside issues of power, privilege and access are central to any research process. However, genuine PAR is difficult for a student to undertake and does not sit comfortably with the additional requirements of an academic programme. Instigated by the community and co-designed by community partners, PAR is time-consuming and may or may not be feasible within the time available to a student researcher. Nor is a student able to influence the pace at which a project moves if adhering properly to the PAR process. While a student may respond to a community request for research they are rarely sufficiently experienced to train community members in research methods and approaches, to co-design research tools and collaboratively carry out the research and analysis and co-write a report. The different levels of expertise among any community group and their aspirations for a project can be challenging for a new researcher to manage.

Given these challenges, it may be more realistic, therefore to support students in collaborative approaches to research, where they start from the interests of a group, benefit from their insight and expertise but retain the freedom to take forward particular elements of the research process. Strand *et al.* (2003) acknowledge the difficulties in managing full participation and suggest that 'at the very least the community should be fully involved in the first phase of the project, identifying research need and designing questions, and in the final phase, of dissemination and implementation' (p. 11). Interrogating the differences between participatory and collaborative research and the benefits and challenges of working with practitioner or indigenous communities is a useful way in to understanding some of the complexities of participation.

Reason and Bradbury (2008) describe PAR as 'a participatory, democratic process concerned with developing practical knowing in the pursuit of worthwhile human purposes, grounded in a participatory world view' (p. 1) and these elements, of participation, reflection, linking theory to practice and dealing with the issues and concerns of local people, are useful as general principles. In practice, however, at Brighton we make a separation between SCE and SCR. The majority of research requests received by the university are more suited to postgraduate students than to undergraduates – who are still very much apprentice researchers. A third-year undergraduate, often learning how to construct a research project for the first time, is generally ill-equipped to deal with the additional complexities of negotiating with a community organisation. However, for a postgraduate, who may be preparing for a career in academia, the opportunity to see research in context is valuable providing the expectations associated with it are made clear from the beginning. The majority of requests for research that have come to Brighton in the past five years have been to evidence need and to evaluate impact and associated with funding bids. In many cases these have more in common with evaluations than with how academia interprets research, nor are they necessarily fitted to community-based or participatory approaches.

As with other areas of our SCE, the SCR strand is underpinned by the core philosophy of mutual benefit and knowledge exchange. Through the provision of a supportive framework and robust processes, each party can be clear about their expectations, working together towards mutually beneficial outcomes. Students are not paid for the work they undertake through SCR. However, if additional costs are incurred for the student whilst carrying out the research, a contribution may be negotiated within the formal agreement drawn up with the community partner.

In identifying appropriate organisations/projects for students to work with, SCR in general apply two principles (adapted from the Living Knowledge website's criteria for science shop clients, www.scienceshops. org):

- Partners may not have the (full) financial means to acquire their research by other means (sometimes applicable questions from these clients are accepted as paid research or research at least subsidised by the client).
- Partners should have no commercial objectives with their question, and the research results must become public (or 'the question must be for the common good').

Key to the process of ensuring successful student research projects are:

- identifying appropriate research questions. Canvasing community partners and gathering a range of research opportunities that might be a good fit with student interests, informing students of the opportunity through dissertation events and having applied research as an optional rather than a compulsory activity.
- finding relevant students. These need to be students who are able to be reasonably flexible about their research

interests but for whom the research project is sufficiently connected with their discipline area.

- managing expectations. Partner expectations of students can be unrealistic in terms of what they may be able to achieve and the impact their research might have within a limited time.
- reaching agreement over the scope and responsibilities of a project.

Time spent in ensuring both parties understand their responsibilities and share a common vision of the project they are working towards is always time well spent. (The Student Community Research Agreement form reproduced earlier is valuable as a way to structure this process.)

References

Baum, F., MacDougall, C. and Smith, D. (2006) 'Participatory action research', *Journal of Epidemiology and Community Health,* 60(10), pp. 854–7.

Blackburn, J. (2000) 'Understanding Paulo Freire, the origins, concepts and possible pitfalls of his educational approach', *Community Development Journal*, 35(1), pp. 3–15.

Bourner, T., Heath, L. and Rospigliosi, A. (2013) 'The fully-functioning university and its higher education', *Higher Education Review*, 45(2), pp. 5–25.

Boyer, E. (1990) *Scholarship Reconsidered: Priorities of the Professorate.* Princetown, NJ: Carnegie Foundation for the Advancement of Teaching.

Dewey, J. (1933) *How We Think: A Restatement of the Relation of Reflective Thinking to the Educative Process.* Boston, MA: D.C. Heath and Company.

Ison, R. (2010) *How to Exist in a Climate Changing World.* Milton Keynes: Open Univerity Press.

Marullo, S. and Edwards, B. (2000) 'From charity to justice, the potential of university-community collaboration for social change', *American Behavioral Scientist*, 43(5), pp. 895–912.

O'Connor, K.M., Lynch, K. and Owen, D. (2011) 'Student-community engagement and the development of graduate attributes', *Education and Training*, 53(2/3), pp.100–115.

Moon, J. (1999) *Reflection in Learning and Professional Development: Theory and Practice.* London: Kogan Page.

Moon, J. (2001) *Reflection in Higher Education/Learning. PDP working paper.* Exeter University.

Moon, J. (2004) *A Handbook of Reflective and Experiential Learning: Theory and Practice.* Abingdon: RoutledgeFalmer.

Moon, J. (2006) *Learning Journals: A Handbook for Reflective Practice and Professional Development*. New York: Routledge.

Moon, J.A. and Learning and Teaching Support Network, Generic Centre (2004) *Reflection and Employability*. York: Learning and Teaching Support Network.

Owen, D. and Hill, S. (2011) *Embedding Public Engagement in the Curriculum, A Framework for the Assessment of Student Learning from Public Engagement*. NCCPE, At: www.publicengagement.ac.uk/sites/default/files/Assessing_student_learning_from_pe.pdf [accessed March 2014].

Reason, P. and Bradbury, H. (2008) *The SAGE Handbook of Action Research: Participative Inquiry and Practice* (2nd edn). London: SAGE.

Schön, D.A. (1987) *Educating the Reflective Practitioner: Toward a New Design for Teaching and Learning in the Professions*. San Francisco: Jossey-Bass.

Stoecker, R. (2003) 'Community based research: From practice to theory and back again', *Michigan Journal of Service Learning*, 9(2), pp. 35–46.

Strand, K. (2003) *Community-Based Research and Higher Education: Principles and Practices*. San Francisco: Jossey-Bass.

CHAPTER SEVEN

Delivering student–community engagement

Introduction

This chapter looks at some of the difficulties that can arise in delivering SCE and offers advice on developing relationships with community partners, supporting students in choosing projects and negotiating different organisational cultures. It draws on the experience of CUPP's community partners and provide suggestions for structuring sessions and managing key debates. It highlights the important role that former students can play in promoting and supporting this work and how experience might be shared between wider student cohorts. It also looks at what can go wrong and ways to mitigate against risk, including some examples of risk assessment processes for different types of activities.

Working with community partners

When working closely with one or two community partners it is easy to keep track of how things are going and the ways in which different students participate. On a larger, cross-university programme with a range of different partners, collecting, brokering and fulfilling opportunities becomes more problematic. Whether sharing a database with the volunteering team, allowing students to find projects through city-based offices or holding a purpose-built database, it is difficult to keep information up to date. Sending students along to projects that have already been filled can be demotivating for them and time-consuming for partners. Leaving opportunities unfilled and community groups waiting for student support that doesn't arrive can damage the reputation of the university. A larger programme needs a good

140

administrative system to ensure that communication is kept up to date and partners have easy access to university personnel.

If the match between a student's interest and an organisation's approach is good then the experience can be hugely beneficial for both of them. When the two are less well aligned or when the student becomes unreliable it quickly reflects badly on students as a whole. It is not uncommon for undergraduates to overestimate their capabilities. Students regularly look for projects in which they can 'help drug addicts' or 'counsel women in a refuge' when their own understanding is under-developed in relation to the reality that these groups have been dealing with for years. While this may be the field in which they are eventually interested in working, any support they can offer without lengthy training and experience is likely to be limited. They are unlikely to be given hands-on work with individuals in difficult or challenging circumstances and may have to choose between routine work in an organisation they want to learn more about; or hands-on work within a more accessible environment. Careful discussion about whether it is more important to develop their skills of working with people, or to take on an administrative task in a rehab or refuge to develop their understanding of context, helps to manage expectations on both sides. Managing expectations of both students and organisations is also necessary to mitigate the danger of disappointment or of someone taking on too much. Students should be made aware of what they might realistically achieve, and what they are able to offer both to an organisation and a client group. Over-promising at the start of a project can cause someone to take on too much responsibility for a situation and put themselves into a situation they find they are unable to handle.

Unrealistic expectations have also led to students complaining that their project work is not sufficiently stretching, with little opportunity to apply theory to practice or develop personally. The organisation may view them as free labour and have them handing out flyers or washing up at community events. If they are able to address this directly with their colleagues and negotiate a different or additional role within the same organisation then that in itself can be more developmental than shifting organisations mid-way through. Supporting them to think through the role and capacity of the group and alternative contributions they might make can lead to creative and innovative projects that would not otherwise have happened. Proper preparation for partners and for students in advance means some of these issues can be avoided. In the early days of a programme holding meetings or one-to-one discussions with community partners is useful in establishing university expectations, as a grounding for the development of longer-term relationships. Scope for refining a module or a community project needs to be built into long-term planning so that as lessons emerge from working together, the university teaching and the community activity might be adapted accordingly.

There a few general principles that can help to minimise misunderstandings:

- *Being honest to partners about the capacity of students and managing their expectations.* It is useful to remind partners in advance of their responsibilities in interviewing supervising and managing a student working with them, that they are free to refuse a student if they feel they are not appropriate but if they do accept them they will need to induct and oversee their work as they would with any employee or volunteer. This may be an undergraduate's first experience in this context and while they may be brilliant they may also struggle with elements of the work that the organisation takes for granted.

- *Encouraging partners to keep in touch with the university and providing them with clear guidelines on what a student's course entails.* A briefing sheet for the organisation, with some explanation of the module, contact details of a tutor and information in advance about any paperwork requirements is a good start but they may need to be reminded of this during the academic year. Keeping a list of student projects and names of local supervisors and emailing them from the university from time to time provides an opportunity for them to get in touch and to deal with any problems as they arise.

- *Requiring students to inform the university as they agree their projects and of any subsequent changes to the project as they work on it.* This means opportunities can be removed from the database as they are filled and supervisors regularly contacted.

- *Checking in with students regularly so that any problems are detected early.* Small tutor groups and close contact between students and tutors is crucial in managing this.

- *Consulting partners for feedback at the end of the year and building their suggestions into a revision of the programme.* For example, as the CUPP programme grew to several hundred a feedback form was emailed to every host organisation, and a quota were also telephoned for a more in depth discussion on how the project went.
- *Inviting partners into the university for an initial matching event or to provide some input into the course and to keep communications open.* Good partnerships are built on personal relationships, if there are multiple forms of contact over a period of time partners are more likely to evolve joint working practices.
- *In complex design or research projects where students are negotiating a final or postgraduate project with partners it can save time to accompany them to a first meeting to ensure all agreements are clear.* The Research Agreement (Chapter Six) has been developed over a number of years and is informed by the experience of a number of partnership struggles.

Boundary-setting in terms of student relationships with client groups should be the responsibility of the organisation hosting the students and the importance of boundaries, of appropriate relationships, and debriefing should be part of any induction programme. There are stringent government regulations surrounding safeguarding and contract with young people and tutors need to ensure that partner organisations are working in accordance with these. Where students are sourcing their own projects, tutors need to keep this as a live part of class discussions in order to ensure it is happening and to provide additional support. Students also need to understand the different working cultures and practices of other institutions and how behaviour, language and dress that might seem as normal in one context can appear inappropriate in another. Where one-to-one client relationships are involved this is particularly important in order to ensure their behaviour and gestures are not misunderstood. Where students are working on research projects with vulnerable groups they will need to go through university ethics review panels and this is dealt with later.

Example

A student working with a group of school children on a holiday project formed close relationships with them during their week together. When she left she shared her Facebook details with some of those she had got to know as a way to keep in touch. A number of the children looked her up when they got home and showed her photograph to their parents. Her Facebook page contained, amongst other things, pictures of her at house parties, drinking and fooling around with her friends. Her parents complained to the school at what they saw as condoning the use of alcohol and inappropriate relationships and the school complained to the university. What the student saw as a small and friendly gesture crossed the boundary between the cultures of different academic institutions where what was acceptable in one context seemed inappropriate in another.

A second student, working in a male prison would go on to her project after morning lectures. One very hot day she arrived at university in a low necked sleeveless t-shirt, which, while normal wear among university students, was not seen as appropriate dress within a male prison. Rather than send her home to change, the prison officer complained to her head of school who reacted by saying she had brought the university into disrepute.

Organisation-based training

Larger civil society organisations often provide their own training which can be hugely developmental to those working with them. The Samaritans, The Citizens' Advice Bureau, The British Trust for Conversation Volunteers and good quality mentoring programmes all provide a significant period of induction and training. Students invariably gain a lot from attending such training and are asked to invest their time in it. This raises the question as to whether it can be counted as part of their designated course hours. Pragmatically, where modules involve a limited commitment of, for example, 30 hours of project work, spending ten of these on training leaves little time for an organisation to benefit from their work. The time and the costs of training a new volunteer only becomes worthwhile for a community group if they can depend on sufficient involvement from a participant in return. This creates a tension between course requirements and organisational responsibilities.

Opening this up for debate among a student group is probably preferable to legislating on it. It is impossible to force a student to continue with a project beyond their agreed university hours and much of their learning and reflection may be based around the training period. However, if the work goes well they may decide to work with the organisation for the rest of their period at university. If training is held late in the term, then students may have no choice but to use this as their practice experience and make an informal commitment to the organisation to continue working with them in the future. Encouraging them to look at the relevance of their community project to other modules on their course, or to pick up an issue within it for their dissertation, can also help to enhance their commitment to the community organisation over and beyond module requirements.

Small organisations that have no formal training programme have a responsibility to induct their staff and students and should be encouraged to use their risk assessments as a check-list to ensure they are aware of fire, equal opportunity, safeguarding and safety procedures. Asking students to feedback on induction processes during a seminar can provide a cue to those who have not been offered them to think about what it is they need to know. Students who are struggling to cope with a practical role can be encouraged to identify an informal mentor they can go to for advice and support. This could be someone within the organisation or a student from an earlier cohort who has undertaken a similar role in the past.

More general but crucial issues of boundary-setting, personal safety, levels of responsibility, line management, debriefing, dealing with conflict, managing time, client communications and so on, can also be covered in class-based discussions.

Using frameworks from action learning and action research

Action learning can be a powerful tool for supporting students on an SCE module and helping them distil the learning from it. Action learning involves learning by developing ideas, testing them out in action, observing the consequences, reflecting on those observations, questioning and, as a result, developing further ideas which, in turn, are tested out in practice and can be summarised through cycles of action and reflection, not dissimilar to Freire's model of praxis.

Figure 7.1. The basic action learning process.

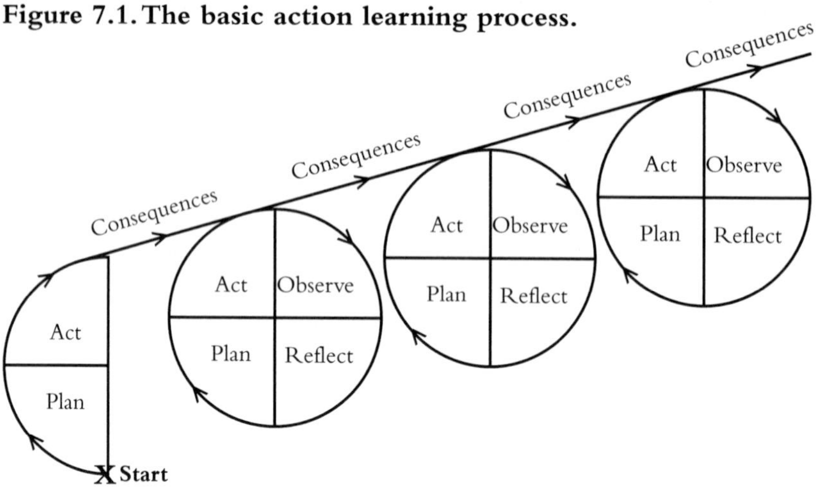

The action learner starts at point 'X' with a wish to tackle some problem, get something done or take action to right some wrong. It then involves the following steps:

1. *Planning* the best action to take given the circumstances
2. Taking *actions* to implement the first part of the plan
3. Looking for *consequences* of the action taken
4. *Observing* carefully the nature of the consequences
5. *Reflecting* on what is observed, drawing conclusions and distilling the lessons

This is the single basic cycle in the action learning process: 1) **P**lanning, 2) Taking **A**ctions, 3) **C**onsequences, 4) **O**bserving, 5) **R**eflecting, or the PACOR cycle.★ This has some similarities with Kolb's experiential learning cycle (1987), with some differences: action learning is a *proactive* process where the learner takes action to create their own experience.

A key element of action learning involves learning through addressing *real issues* as opposed to case studies or scenarios that have been constructed for a learning process (Simpson and Bourner, 2007). It is learning that goes beyond solving purely intellectual puzzles to include

★ This concept was developed through the writing of this chapter but has since been written up in Bourner, T. and Simpson, P. (forthcoming) 'Action learning and the pedagogy of professional Doctorates', *Higher Education, Skills and Work Based Learning.*

action to test whether possible solutions actually work in the real world. This often amounts to testing whether the world is as the learner understands it to be and whether the learner is as they think they are. In other words, it can generate self-knowledge as well as knowledge about the world (see Bourner's domains of learning in Chapter 4). The process is dependent on peer support through establishing small action learning sets, and when effective these support and encourage reflection. The action learning set or small group becomes a safe space to explore the challenges emerging from SCE projects, encouraging individuals in turn to look at the alternative courses of action open to them in a particular situation and the impact of their behaviour on others. Through the creation of safe and supportive spaces in which group members can be open about themselves and the difficulties they may be experiencing, there are significant opportunities for personal and professional learning.

Typically, an action learning set will comprise half a dozen learners with a member of staff to facilitate the process, but small groups can be formed which meet alongside each other in a bigger tutor facilitated session. The groups need to meet at regular intervals and facilitators should ensure that during the meeting each of the members gets an equal share of the time available. Group members should be encouraged to use the time they have available to explore how their project is going and to reflect on their experience since the last meeting, identifying difficulties they are encountering and the options they have for addressing these. During these discussions the group supports each member to decide on their best course of action in order to address these issues before the group meets again. One person acts as note-taker each week and records the actions for each member, and the tutor acts as time-keeper in order to ensure that the time available is allocated evenly. Each learner will leave the meeting with a set of action points to be completed by the next meeting when these will again be reviewed by the set, and it is this focus on action and reflection that supports learning. The quality and depth of the learning is dependent on the groups' level of skill in asking questions and the willingness of each member to be open and to risk. The bigger the commitment a student is able to make to the process, the deeper the learning. However, it requires a student to be willing to make themselves vulnerable within this context – to engage and share their vulnerabilities and undergraduates in particular find this challenging. A skilled tutor can facilitate and foster this process, but without it class contributions can be stilted and learning less deep.

With the right support the ability to share experience and to learn from each other, however, can be a valuable tool in SCE modules. There are a range of resources available to guide the introduction of action learning sets with exercises for training students in how to use them and examples of useful questions (see, for example, Pedlaer and Abbott, 2013).

Action research and the co-creation of knowledge

Action research (along with CBR, PAR and action learning) is a useful concept to introduce in relation to participatory working and the co-production of knowledge. Chapter One of this book discusses the difference as outlined by Gibbons *et al.* of Mode 1 knowledge (that is abstract, conceptual and decontextualised) and Mode 2 knowledge (that is applied, contextualised and drawn from practice). Community–university partnerships and action research approaches often refer to the co-creation of knowledge – bringing together different modes of knowledge for a holistic understanding of context that is informed by concepts and experience. While this is often referred to as the application of theory to practice, the co-creation of knowledge is more than this and looks at the new knowledge that can be generated by different groups working together. Chapter Four of this book also introduced a series of questions to promote different forms of thinking, looking at the difference between critical thinking (which often underlies Mode 1 knowledge) and reflective thinking (that can lead to Mode 2 knowledge). Introducing students to different forms of knowledge, the equal value of different types of knowledge, and what can be gained from bringing the experience of practitioners to bear on the more theoretical or conceptual knowledge of academics, can help them to make sense of community engagement principles.

Unpacking options of voluntarism, welfare and rights-based approaches to delivery

In the UK we have largely rejected the US term 'service learning' because of the service and welfare connotations it carries. However, Iles, writing about a project in Roehampton, London in 'Service learning and reflective practice' (in McIlrath and MacLabhrainn [2007]) defends the use of the term it shifts students away from thinking about their work purely with regard to the experience they can gain for themselves. She suggests providing students with reading around notions of service and reciprocity, to explore these values at an early point in the course can help students engage with notions of service critically. Kari and Skelton in 'Place matters: Partnerships for civic learning' (also in MacIlrath [2007]) discuss the difference between a service and an organising approach to community work. Whereas a service (or welfare) models tries to 'fix' problems, serve individuals and clients and implement short-term projects, a rights-based approach is more concerned with building power through networks and building capacity in the community to mobilise the changes they want to bring about. Marullo and Edwards (2000) and Stoecker (2009) differentiate between charity and social justice approaches to community work and these were explored earlier in this chapter. Whatever approach is taken by an SCE programme it is useful to unpack with students' questions of voluntarism, welfare and rights-based approaches to service provision.

Marullo and Edwards suggest six key areas for discussion with students about the projects in which they are working:

1. Does the organisation reflect the voices of those who use it in the way that it operates? Does it have an equal opportunities policy?
2. Does the module encourage students to examine root causes of social problems rather than just alleviating their impact on individuals?
3. Are students given the opportunity to examine broader political, social and institutional context in which social problems are situated?
4. Are their sufficient links with other modules in a course programme to build on the understandings developed in this one?
5. Are individual students supported in addressing personal challenges and building strong community relationships?
6. Does the way partnerships are brokered and managed reflect the principles of transparency, equity and diversity? (adapted from Marullo [2000])

These six questions suggest ways in which students can be supported to move from an individual to a structural understanding of social problems, to a deeper knowledge and an exploration of how they can work for social change.

In Brighton we have explored these areas with students in different ways, as follows.

Values and aspirations: Early sessions in a module have looked at the student's own aspirations for the future through examining a series of statements made by high profile figures (for example, Mandela, King, Thatcher, Blair) about their values. Without knowing the author of each statement, students are asked to walk around the room and identify those that most relate to their own view and then discuss where this view stems from with anyone else who has chosen similarly. Seminars include discussions on the changing approaches to community work, notions of participation and power and the status of different forms of knowledge.

Others have looked at articles on citizenship or the involvement of young people in political issues as a way to shift more familiar, textual analysis, to a personal exploration of the issues addressed in the text. Deconstructing such an article (using some of Bourner's questions for critical thinking) can quickly open up discussions about what students know or believe to be true and where these beliefs come from.

Charity and social justice: An example used in some US programmes is Illich's essay 'To Hell with good intentions' (an address given to the conference on Inter-American Student projects). It offers a harsh criticism of the paternalism of international volunteers in 1968 but has relevance for local students working on current programmes by citing the damage that can be created by young people who volunteer with little awareness of the culture and context in which they are working. Encouraging students to reflect on how their perception of a particular community changes, what they learn from whom, and the dangers of a deficit model (focusing on what an individual or a community lacks rather than the strengths and resource they have) helps to deepen their understanding of mutuality.

> *Next to money and guns, the third largest North American export is the U.S. idealist, who turns up in every theatre of the world: the teacher, the volunteer, the missionary, the community organizer, the economic developer, and the vacationing do-gooders. Ideally, these people define their role as service. Actually, they frequently wind up alleviating the damage done by money and weapons, or 'seducing' the 'underdeveloped' to the benefits of the world of affluence and achievement.* (Illich, 1968)

150

Learning from communities: Starting with a discussion of language and terms can also be useful in understanding the difference between voluntarism and reciprocity, welfare and advocacy, projects and placements and the appropriate language to describe this work. Students can be introduced to their own learning styles and preferences, the different ways in which they have learned different things in their lives and the relative significance of these. Looking at how the language we use frames the way we think about things can be useful for a humanities student while an analysis of the responsibilities of state and citizens or the rise of social inequality can have more meaning for a social science student. Scientists often prefer to start with discussing the way knowledge is used in society, who has access to it and how it is created, disseminated and shared.

Grasping the concept of reciprocity and mutual benefit takes time and it's not unusual for students on engaged modules to move from an over-concern with themselves to an over-concern with those using the projects they work with. Undergraduates often follow a pattern, beginning with very little confidence and a real worry as to whether they have anything to contribute to feeling they can change the world – or at the very least the life of the young person they are working with. Invariably this leads to disappointment when things don't quite work and when the world, or the individual, is reluctant to be changed. Communities may reject or challenge the 'help' that a young undergraduate feels they are able to offer seeing them as privileged or out of touch with local realities. Supporting a student through this process to a more realistic sense of their own place in the world is an important part of SCE, as is the understanding of the contested and often unhelpful notion of a 'helping' approach.

Drawing on mentors and alumni and establishing a community of practice

Former students, working as advocates or mentors, can be invaluable in introducing the concept of SCE to a new group through speaking about their own experience and becoming part of a community of practice to develop thinking about engagement. Often it is only some time after completing community-based work that students realise its significance and how much it has taught them and become strong advocates for what at the time seemed a challenging experience. In Brighton, former students have been inspirational speakers in the early weeks of seminars when new students are still trying to grasp what seems to be a very different way of working. They have been invited into whole-group induction lectures to talk about their projects or asked to attend small seminar groups and action learning sets to facilitate more in-depth discussions.

Where degree courses have integrated engaged learning into first, second and third years, we have been able to use third years to take a leadership and mentoring role with new students. Working in this way enables final-year students to build on the legacy of their project, often taking their second-year projects to new levels and incorporating new students into the programme. Developing the interpersonal skills to support a new student and act as a mentor can also be valuable training for someone hoping to go on to a management role within a future career. Business school modules have used this approach effectively with the third-year SCE option including a leadership element so students can validate their leadership potential.

Finding ways to keep in touch with students as they move through modules can provide an important teaching resource as well as indications of the longer-term impact of SCE on future life choices. Keeping contact with alumni also opens up possibilities for researching and evidencing the long-term effects of engaged learning. Research into how far engagement contributes to long-term attitudes to citizenship or life choices and work opportunities is limited, and while many claims are made for its impact, there has been little longitudinal research. *Bursting the Bubble* (Brewis, Russell and Holdsworth, 2010) charts the experience of 6000 graduates in relation to the benefits of volunteering, in terms of how they felt they had benefitted from it in their future lives. Anecdotal evidence indicates that some students go on to work for local charities and, in turn, provide project opportunities for future students on SCE modules from the university. However, such evidence tends to have been gathered from chance meetings or initiated by students contacting the university to look for references. However, there is huge potential for more systematic research if contacts with former students can be maintained. The NCCP encourages all participating universities to email alumni about the impact of engagement of their future careers (www.publicengagement.ac.uk/how/guides/survey-questions).

In Brighton we have tried to do this in a number of ways. These have included:

- collecting student numbers of individuals on SCE modules and tracking these against first destination statistics to see if there is a correlation between participating in SCE and finding work (see Millican and Bourner, 2011);
- encouraging new students to join a Facebook page set up to support them through SCE and using this as a mechanism to contact students in the future and to keep in touch with their changing career paths;
- inviting all students to join the CUPP network on completion of the module (http//:cuppcoppning.org) and organising these into a single SCE group; and
- working with module leaders in different schools to create personal email lists of students that will be live when their university contacts have expired.

Requests from former students have also raised issues about the possibility of providing mentoring to graduates who are keen to move on into work in civil society organisations. The CUPP team have a background in developmental work, design and management of projects, securing funding for community projects and in evaluating project ideas. They are also connected to a network of colleagues and organisations with extensive experience in this field. Making this available to new graduates just starting out in this field, in return for them sharing their own experiences with new students, seems an equally valuable form of reciprocity.

Between 2010 and 2012 CUPP ran a postgraduate internship programme, using an open Masters framework to provide accreditation for a three-month period spent working on a particular project for a local voluntary organisation. The Masters programme, an independent study programme offered 'by learning objectives' required students to write their own learning objectives for their work and to specify, in negotiation with the supervisor, the appropriate assessment for this work. By using the 60-credit exit award available for students finishing early, they were able to create a postgraduate certificate 'by internship'. Organisations were invited to submit internship projects which ranged from creating a series of handbooks and policies which helped an organisation gain an 'Investors in People award', to conducting an extensive piece of research on the users of a wood recycling service. In each case students were based within the organisation concerned for at least three days a week and provided with a desk, line supervision and the status of a part-time employee. The organisation paid the university fee for the postgraduate certificate and interns attended the university one day a fortnight for seminars on leadership and project management and to participate in action learning sets. In return for three months intensive work, interns gained a postgraduate qualification, valuable experience in the field and a range of contacts established during their role. Organisations gained a substantial piece of work that had been scrutinised by academic partners for the cost of a few hundred pounds in student fees. In a number of cases interns went on to gain full-time positions within the organisations in which they were based.

However, over time the cost of a postgraduate certificate went up and voluntary organisations found it difficult to afford them. In addition students increasingly struggled with supporting themselves through a three-month internship without pay. For a while government policy allowed graduates who had been unemployed for six months to take on an internship while claiming benefits and the programme was shifted to January in order to accommodate this cohort. However, as policies changed again, this opportunity was removed. CUPP experimented with offering a shorter-term opportunity attached to a 20-postgraduate module, but without the currency of a PGCert., or the quality of experience attached to a three-month internship, this did not attract the same number of interested students.

Risk-assessment, insurance and ethical procedures for SCR

From our experience, encouraging students to carry out their own risk-assessments, and designing these together, might have a better chance of preventing harm than tick-box exercises imposed by the university. Each project will have different elements of danger that a generic risk-assessment may miss. Including a specific risk-assessment exercise, some confirmation of the training or induction undertaken can be built into the sign-off process for any new student project. An example of a risk-assessment exercise developed by a tutor at Brighton is included below. The purpose of this is not to replace an institutional form already in use by the organisation but to encourage students to be aware of the risks they may cause and encounter while there.

154

Example

Community participation and development							
Student's name		Signature			Date assessed		
Project location							
What are the hazards?	Who may be harmed?	What controls are already in place?	Risk rating	Additional controls required to reduce risk	Risk rating	Date action taken and by whom	
			Low Medium High		Low Medium High		
			Low Medium High		Low Medium High		
			Low Medium High		Low Medium High		
			Low Medium High		Low Medium High		
Emerging risk		Action taken				Date	

Guidance to accompany student risk assessment form

You should be aware of health and safety risks that you may encounter when working on projects outside of the University. The organisation that you are working for should have carried out a H&S risk assessment as part of their organisation's management processes – but it is good practice for you, when going into situations, to do this yourself.

You need to ask yourself four basic questions:

1. What are the hazards involved in my placement?
   - Falls
   - Lifting
   - Machinery
   - Hazardous substances
   - Violence & aggression
2. What harm may I (or someone else) come to?
3. What is the likelihood of this happening?
4. What can be done to reduce the impact/risk?

You are likely to find that the organisation will already have measures in place to reduce some of the general issues – it is good to ask the questions about these when completing your H&S questionnaire. You will need to think particularly about the specific risks that you may face in the activities you carry out in the course of your placement.

The form above will help you with this. Complete the columns as follows:

1. List the potential hazards – add further rows if necessary.
2. List who may be harmed (it could be people who you are working with).
3. List the existing controls (precautions) that have already been put into place by the organisation.
4. Rate the level of risk (low, medium or high) after the organisation's controls are taken into account.

5. Describe the actions and measures that you are taking to limit the risk.
6. Reassesses the level of risk now that you have added in your own controls.
7. Give a date - and state who took the action.

In the space at the bottom of the form you can note any hazards that you become aware of as you do your project – and the actions you take.

The accepted rule is to be *risk-aware*, not *risk-averse* – in other words, be aware of what the risks are and take careful precautions – only in extreme cases is it necessary to say, 'I can't do that'.

Taken from the Health & Safety Executive website: www.hse. gov.uk/risk/faq.htm

What is a hazard? A hazard is anything with the potential to cause harm e.g. working at height on scaffolding.
What is risk? A risk is the likelihood that a hazard will cause a specified harm to someone or something, e.g. if there are no guard rails on the scaffolding it is likely that a construction worker will fall and break a bone.
What is risk management? Risk management is a process that involves assessing the risks that arise in your workplace, putting sensible health and safety measures in place to control them and then making sure they work in practice.
What is risk assessment? A risk assessment is nothing more than a careful examination of what, in your work, could cause harm to people, so that you can weigh up whether you have taken enough precautions or should do more to prevent harm.

Further help at: 'Five steps to risk assessment': www.hse.gov.uk/ pubns/indg163.pdf

Example of a risk assessment form to be completed by organisations accepting students:

Health and Safety

The Health and Safety at Work legislation requires the University to ensure student placements are made only with organisations who take health and safety seriously; and that account will be taken of the student's youth or inexperience.

- Does the organisation have a written safety policy?
- Is the registered with the charity commission or local authority?
- Have you been offered a period of induction to cover health and safety arrangements, including fire precautions, specific hazards and health and safety precautions?
- Will you be offered appropriate guidance or training in work practices and in the particular task you will be doing including a risk assessment?
- Will you or the organisation notify the University of any accidents or incidents that involve your safety?
- Is the organisation required to have employers liability (compulsory insurance)?
- Does the organisation hold a current certificate and public liability insurance?
- Does the organisation have an equal opportunities policy (if it has more than four employees?)
- Please add the address of the site where your placement will be undertaken.
- Please indicate if there are any health restrictions or medical fitness requirements associated with the task you will be undertaking.

In ten years of running engaged modules there have been no great disasters. The most common student problems have included delays in project start dates, so that hours cannot be completed within module deadlines, delays in the process for Criminal Record Bureau checks, a student being refused on a project because of a past offence or an organisation forced to close due to finances. In each case, students have been encouraged to choose new roles or activities, combine reflections on different roles in their assignments and/or given extensions on their submission dates. The most common problems experienced by community organisations have arisen from students not properly understanding the culture of the context in which they are working and what counts as appropriate behaviour. On the whole, these difficulties are rare and most students rise to the challenges they are presented with, assuming responsibility for children, adults, buildings or animals placed into their care.

In an extreme case, if something did go wrong a student should be covered by the public liability insurance of the organisation in which they work. Verifying this with an organisation is an important part of the risk assessment process, and students should be required to ensure that their public liability insurance is up to date. This should cover students for all eventualities unless they are at fault in an issue of negligence or the university has been negligent in their care towards them. This might be if a student were knowingly put into a situation which is dangerous for them or those that are left in their care, or where one party withholds information about, for example, a previous conviction or an undue risk. Where this is the case and the university is legally liable, the university's insurance policy should cover legal or personal costs incurred.

Ethics review processes

Postgraduate students undertaking community-based research as part of their final dissertations or supplementary modules will need to consider ethical review processes if they are working with vulnerable communities. While without strong ethics approval and relevant security checks, they will be banned with working with young people under the age of 18 in any capacity, with other groups the boundaries will appear more blurred. A proper ethics review process is designed to ensure the security of both students and research participants, and is a valuable process for students to learn. These often take time. With students trying to complete a piece of academic research in line with a strict timetable, this time can make a difference between a student meeting or missing a deadline and a subsequent exam board. It is important, therefore, if tutors are considering incorporating SCR into an academic programme that ample time is given for this. It is often helpful to introduce students to dissertation areas in the year prior to dissertations being written so that these processes can be put underway and relevant contacts and applications made.

It also raises a broader issue of power and ownership and who decides what is and what is not acceptable. Community organisations often feel they know their clients and those they work with, and are reluctant to accept a university decision that a piece of work may be unacceptable.

Ethics review processes are also often built around medical models of research and are not open to including community partners in their decision-making bodies. Participant information sheets and consent forms, required by academic institutions, can seem prohibitive and off-putting to individuals who may struggle with literacy or with the conventions of a university and create more fear than they are designed to allay.

Both the University of Brighton (Faculty of Arts) and the University of Durham (Centre for Justice and Community) have worked on processes that are both fair and inclusive and designed to enable consent to be gained from people who may have literacy or learning difficulties and enable review panels to understand more about the realities of community based research. These can be found at www.arts.brighton. ac.uk/__data/assets/pdf_file/0005/58739/Faculty-Ethics-guidelines. pdf, and www.engage-nu.com/wp-content/uploads/2013/11/ Ethics-in-community-based-participatory-research–Case-studies-case-examples-and-commentaries.pdf respectively.

References

Banks, S. and Armstrong, A. (2010) *Ethics in Community-Based Participatory Research: Case Studies, Case Examples and Commentaries.* NCCPE, www. engage-nu.com/wp-content/uploads/2013/11/Ethics-in-community-based-participatory-research-Case-studies-case-examples-and-commenta ries.pdf [accessed March 2014].

Bourner, T. and Millican, J. (2011) 'Student–community engagement and graduate employability', *Widening Participation and Lifelong Learning*, 13(2), pp. 68–85.

Brewis, G., Russell, J. and Holdsworth, C. (2010) *Bursting the Bubble; Students, Volunteering and The Community.* VInspired Students, the Institute for Volunteering Research and the NCCPE. At: https://www.publicengagement. ac.uk/sites/default/files/NCCPE%20-%20Bursting%20the%20bubble_0_0. pdf [accessed March 2014].,

Fox, A. (2010) *Ethical Research Guidelines for Staff and Students.* Faculty of Arts, University of Brighton. At: arts.brighton.ac.uk/__data/assets/pdf_ file/0005/58739/Faculty-Ethics-guidelines.pdf [accessed October 2014]

Illich, I. (1968) *To Hell with Good Intentions.* Talk Delivered at the Conference on Inter-American Student Projects, Cuernavaca, Mexico, 20 April 1968. At: www.alterinfos.org/spip.php?article5168 [accessed March 2014].

Marullo, S. and Edwards, B. (2000) 'From charity to justice, the potential of university-community collaboration for social change', *American Behavioral Scientist* 43(5), pp. 895–912.

McIlrath, L. and MacLabhrainn, I. (eds) (2007) *Higher Education and Civic Engagement: International Perspectives*. Farnham: Ashgate.

Pedler, M. and Abbott, C. (2013) *Facilitating Action Learning*. Milton Keynes: Open University Press.

Stoecker, R. (2003) 'Community Based Research: From practice to theory and back again', *Michigan Journal of Service Learning*, 9(2), pp. 35–46.

CHAPTER EIGHT

Assessing student–community engagement

Introduction

This chapter discusses how to create an assessment framework for SCE. It itemises the key areas of learning from an SCE programme and suggests how each of these might be assessed. It looks at the main problems in accurately assessing learning and explores how they might be resolved, highlighting the difference between assessing experience and assessing learning from experience and the concept of 'deep' learning within the process of reflection. It draws some lessons from the assessment of work-based learning and critical thinking that are relevant to SCE and provides examples of different assessment tasks.

Developing an assessment framework

SCE, like community–university engagement more generally, is based on the principle of reciprocity, aiming to be mutually beneficial to students and to the community organisations in which they are based. Stoecker and Tyron (2009) criticise those projects that promote learning but ignore the needs of the community group, treating local neighbourhoods as a laboratory in which students might undertake their learning without sufficient regard for those that inhabit them. A successful SCE programme depends on the identification of learning opportunities for students that meet a real need within the locality and provide some scope for personal development (see Owen, 2012). The learning that results could involve all four of the domains of knowledge outlined in Bourner's table (in Chapter Four): Knowledge about the world; Skills of acting in the world; Knowledge of self; and Skills in managing self in relation to others.

In practice most professional work, including that of a researcher, involves the understanding and application of theoretical principles or discipline-based knowledge, intra- and interpersonal skills and the changing priorities of organisational and national policies. SCE introduces students to the way in which these areas interact and the tensions between them. Assessment of SCE enables experiential work to be accredited and provides feedback to students on their ability to capture and make sense of their learning and to work effectively with an awareness of theory, policy and context.

Learning outcomes that have been specified for a course require a corresponding assessment task to certify that they have been achieved. Assessment confers legitimacy on an activity and, despite any attempt to focus primarily on the value of the learning experience, it is the assessment of that learning experience that encourages people to take it seriously. There are parallels to be drawn here with work-based learning which, until secure methods of assessment for learning were developed, remained on the margins of HE. SCE will not achieve full legitimacy as an approach to learning until the method of assessment is seen to be secure.

In 2011, Owen and Hill, as part of the National Coordinating Centre for Public Engagement in the UK, prepared an assessment framework for public engagement that could be used as a guide for universities in developing engaged work. While these were developed at Level 6 (second-year undergraduate) the principles they include can be adapted and mapped onto higher levels of achievement. They are intended to be cross-curricular in nature and to assess the broader skills that are not covered in discipline-related study. They encourage faculty to map existing learning outcomes against the broad areas of:

- co-creation of knowledge
- managing engagement
- awareness of self and others
- communication
- reflective practice

The framework develops learning outcomes and corresponding assessment criteria for each of these areas. It is available on the NCCPE website (www.nccpe.org.uk) and provides a valuable starting point for academics assessing engaged work. Written for public rather than social or community engagement, the criteria are concerned with working across practice boundaries, managing projects, developing empathy, communicating effectively and learning from reflection. They don't include an analysis of how power is used or transferred, or an awareness of organisational structures and policies. However, they are a useful starting point for resolving some of the difficulties that arise in practice from assessing the various elements of SCE and these are discussed more broadly below.

The areas for assessment

Experience in Brighton has brought to light a number of areas that have proved more difficult to assess. Some of these areas are touched upon in Owen and Hill's framework and include:

1. Mutual benefit, the contribution to the community from the project, a student's attitude and involvement with a community group, their awareness and ability to work with different forms of knowledge and to learn from others (including the co-creation of knowledge).

2. The application of discipline-related theory to practice, an understanding of how theoretical concepts or discipline-based knowledge might be applied in practical situations, the ability to communicate these effectively with different groups (including communication).

3. An understanding of policy, how policy is created and changed and how this might compromise theoretical principle or impact on practice, an awareness of the importance of context and the location of learning in context, of issues of governance, how organisations are structured and how decisions are made (working in complex and interconnected environments, also in the management of engagement).

4. The skills of empathy or affective learning, an understanding of self and the ability to respond to others, to work effectively in teams, to manage emotions – (including awareness of self and others).

5. The ability to learn from experience by reflecting on experience, deep learning, autonomy (or the skills of reflective practice).

Working in each of these areas can be problematic in different ways, as follows.

1. Mutual benefit, providing something of value to the community you are working with, the co-creation of knowledge. Gibbon's differentiation between Mode 1 knowledge (scientific and context-free) and Mode 2 knowledge production (context-based, problem-focused and applied) (1994) similarly relates to Bourner's four domains, the ability to see and use both decontextualised scientifically produced knowledge and the new knowledge that emerges out of practice and from the skills of working within the world. Chapter Seven ('Action research and the co-creation of knowledge' section) discussed the co-creation of knowledge that brings together academic and practitioner skills, applying and seeing the value of knowledge in context. Assessment of an SCE programme is concerned with how far students have been able to own and to apply knowledge, to bring together different types of knowledge and to construct meaning from them.

Assessing students' ability to understand and to use contextually produced knowledge, to apply their knowledge about the world to specific situations and to learn from the people they are working among requires a different approach to that used in traditional academic programmes and a personal rather than an objective voice in assignments. In work-based learning, workplace assessors would be trained to evaluating a student's performance on placement and university co-coordinators may be employed to visit students. In a single SCE module this is rarely realistic. Students find themselves opportunities in a range of community-based organisations playing a variety of different roles. Some of these may be offered year on year to each new cohort, while others emerge according to need as one-off tasks. The evaluation at the University of Brighton above showed that some community partners would like to see the learning outcomes that students are assessed against. Some have also added valuable insights into these outcomes, based on their experiences of working with students. The involvement at this level can also help with their agency/power and ability to influence the programme. There may be neither the funding to employ someone to visit students in their projects nor a will among community organisations to train as assessors. In Brighton, organisations are asked to provide a 'sign off sheet' to show a student has completed their required number of hours on a project, and are invited to give feedback on how it went but it would not seem fair to grade a student against this feedback, generated in such different organisational contexts.

There are also occasions when projects fail, sometimes due to factors outside of a student's control. Even when a student is implicated in a project going wrong, in an experiential learning situation the learning often occurs after mistakes have happened. Unlike a traditional course, where students are 'taught' in a relatively safe environment and then assessed on what they are taught, experiential learning 'teaches' through experience, and there is often more to be learned from situations that have gone wrong than from those that have been a success. If a student is to be assessed on their learning rather than their performance, the focus of their assessment needs to be on 'mutual benefit', on their understanding of what they and their partners have gained from the activity and what might be done differently a second time. While this could be assessed through reflective assignments it may also be possible to assess a practical task which is achieved for the benefit of the organisation and submitted as evidence of achievement. An example of this is a filmed presentation given to the organisation prior to leaving, outlining the work or project the student has led within it and ensuring that any learning gained from the activity is embedded in staff for the long term once a student leaves.

2. *The application of theory to practice and the ability to communicate complex knowledge in practical situations.* Lecturers are often keen to use SCE as an opportunity to apply course-related theory to practical situations, and to use knowledge gained from their course in a practice situation. Tying this into an assessment task helps to ensure that students are able to relate theory to practice and sets up the habit of using existing research to understand new situations better. The field of work-based learning has legitimised the practice of learning logs in HE, structured in a way that requires students to respond to particular aspects of their work. These can be presented in the form of a pre-produced booklet, asking students to write about occasions when they used a particular approach or were able to apply an idea to a specific situation. Such logs can guide student reflection requiring an analysis of a set of theoretical principles encouraging students to reflect on the way in which theory informed their practice or supported a decision they made. But there are occasions where an obvious link between theory and practice is not apparent and where jumping through assessment hoops to identify one may seem something of a meaningless task.

166

Alternatively, students can be asked to write their own reflective account that includes, for example, an analysis of a situation that went well and one that went badly with some theoretical underpinning to illustrate the difference between the two. A dental student learning how to deal with children on a holiday project for example, or a mathematics student working for an animal charity may gain valuable learning without being able to apply learning direct from their discipline area. Assessment tasks need to be broad enough to specific theoretical application of discipline related work where it is assured but allow students to reflect on broader theoretical principles if this is not the case. Interrogating students' understanding of what 'theory' means and about the cognitive, behavioural and affective learning outcomes associated with a particular module, and their value, is not a bad place to start.

SCE projects bring students into contact with different groups and the ability to communicate with these groups and to communicate with a range of audiences is a core part of many programmes. Students on SCR or research modules may need to create a separate report on recommendations, or summary of findings for an organisation's use over and above the academic research report they provide for their normal module assessment, or be willing to give a presentation to employees or board members about the learning from their work. Adding a learning outcome associated with sharing findings, or preparing material to a brief specified by an outside organisation can develop habits of communicating complex ideas in accessible language and can be additional to the submission of a longer dissertation or essay. Some research modules require students to submit, for example, a 6000-word report *and* a summary for the organisation, or to compile an academic essay *and* to prepare a separate communication for a local group.

An awareness of the significance of language and the different languages used by both academic and community group has been an important part of learning how to operate community–university partnerships. Both universities and voluntary organisations use a plethora of acronyms as short hand for what are familiar internal terms, systems and policies but often unknown by outsiders. Partnership working entails being acutely aware of how these are used as well as the ability to explain terms and to use them appropriately.

However in SCE it seems equally important not to require students to 'jump through assessment hoops' and a practical task, prepared to communicate the outcome of the project to a broader community group can also be used as an assessed piece. As long as common assessment criteria and learning outcomes can be identified for a student group these can be applied to different practice based tasks.

Tasks assessing the relation of theory to practice or the ability to communicate discipline related knowledge could include:

- a structured learning log with prepared boxes asking a student to identify instances where particular ideas might be applied;
- an executive report from a longer academic piece of research outlining key recommendations for the organisation and suggesting ways in which these might be implemented;
- a presentation to the board on a piece of research that has been undertaken followed by a discussion with them on how this might be undertaken, filmed and submitted for assessment; and
- guidelines written for users on how to operate a piece of specially designed software or application, assessed alongside the designed work.

These could be accompanied by some critical reflection on the effectiveness of different communication styles, negotiation with community partners on how they would like work presented or feedback from an audience on how useable they found the material produced.

3. *Understanding of how policy is related to practice, the management of engagement.* Constructing a learning outcome that links policy to practice encourages students to unpack the relationship between the two and encourages a deeper understanding of how policy operates. Assignments can be related to organisational policy or national policy but serve to link an experiential piece of work to a particular organisational, geographical or chronological context. The nature of policy context and how far it impacts on a student project is likely to vary and an assessment task needs to test an awareness of what policy is and how it operates with some form of evaluation of how far it has impacted on practice over time. Students might be encouraged to interview longer-serving employees about how the policy context has changed, and to research a particular policy initiative and how this has made a difference

168

to the way people work. Assignments can be structured using a critical or comparative approach or built into a longer guided reflection.

Understanding bias and how perspectives are framed by different contexts, how power operates to include and to exclude and how decisions are made, are all important elements in working effectively with different groups, as is understanding the impact of policy on practice.

Students are often asked to show an understanding of the organisational context in which they are working, the structure and the culture of their organisation, how it is funded and governed and how decisions are made. Providing an organisational analysis requires the application of organisational theory to an observed situation and a deeper interrogation of the key players in a particular field. This might include consideration of the role of the voluntary and the statutory sector, the difference between voluntary and commercial organisations, the challenges a particular sector faces in undertaking this kind of work. It helps students to place their observations of work being done by an organisation into the context of the restrictions and requirements externally placed on that work. Understanding how these impact on different work environments is valuable learning for graduates who are beginning to consider where they might work in the future, and may be looking to explore how their own value set fits among potential employers and which employers might employ someone with their range of skills.

Tasks linked to an analysis of policy could include:

- a critical review of developments in policy over the past five/ten years;
- an interrogation of national policy relating to this context and an evaluation of how or whether it has impacted on a particular client group;
- internal research within an organisation into how employees or clients are aware of organisational mission statements or health and safety policies and the way these are developed and communicated;
- a reflective piece with examples of how policy might impact on practice in different situations;
- an organisational analysis using organisational theory to interrogate the structure and culture of an organisation and to compare it to groups doing similar work from other sectors; and

- the creation of a handbook for future volunteers in an organisation – outlining the procedures, processes, policies and mission statement with advice on how to approach or work with clients.

4. *Empathy and affective learning, awareness of self and others.* The early twenty-first century saw a growing concern with emotional literacy and the understanding that successful projects are made and broken by the interpersonal abilities of those working within them. Matthews (2006) discusses the difference between emotional intelligence (the ability to understand others) and emotional literacy (the ability to respond appropriately in particular cultural and contextual situations). In an article written with Snowdon in 2007, defending the introduction of emotional literacy to educational programmes, he quotes Weare:

> The ability to understand ourselves and other people, and in
> particular to be aware of, understand, and use information about the
> emotional states of ourselves and others with competence. It includes
> the ability to understand, express and manage our own emotions and
> respond to the emotions of others, in ways that are helpful to ourselves
> and others. (Weare, 2003, p. 2)

Matthews's and Snowden's research provides evidence of the value of introducing emotional literacy into science lessons, showing how secondary school pupils enjoy lessons more and support each other in their learning, and suggests there would be a similar value to university students. Making students aware of how they work in groups and support each other is valuable preparation for effective team working in academic and professional situations. Negotiating with others, taking initiative, moving outside of their comfort zone, making decisions and completing practical tasks, an awareness of personal work preferences, and the ability to identify and change negative behaviours, are all elements of emotional literacy that can be identified and tracked. However, grading students as a group on the completion of a group task invariably penalises some and advantages others. SCE programmes have experimented with peer assessment (in action learning sets) and group-to-group assessments (groups observing or commenting on group presentations), and these have been more and less successful in different areas. While students are generally happy to contribute to group presentations and provide

170

feedback on each other's contribution to a task, they generally prefer tutor feedback on their work and an individual grade.

Learning outcomes associated with assessing emotional literacy could include:

- awareness of own ability to negotiate, take responsibility, deal with risk and manage collaborative working;
- awareness of personal development during this module and how values and attitudes have changed; and
- ability to work individually and in a group and to support others in their development and learning.

Assessment criteria could include:
- clear contextual detail with an understanding of the multiple perspectives of the different actors and ability to interpret different values systems that have influenced these;
- strong awareness of how attitudes, values and emotions have developed over the course of the module with an analysis of factors leading to this change; and
- critical reflection on own strengths and weaknesses in relation to individual and group working with clear strategies for how to develop these in the future.

Many of these can be assessed through a reflective essay or a regular blog with a final summary statement.

5. *Reflective practice*
Developing students' capacity for reflective learning is part of developing their capacity to learn how to learn. Reflective learning has also become increasingly important in postgraduate programmes where it is often combined with taught and research elements. According to the Quality Assurance Agency for Higher Education (QAAHE),

> *Progression within postgraduate study has traditionally implied an increasingly narrow, and increasingly research-dependent deepening of knowledge in a specific field. The Harris Review ... however, noted that the distinction between taught, research and reflective elements of postgraduate study had become blurred and that programmes were*

increasingly combining two or more of these elements. (QAAHE, 1998, p. 4)

The emergence of large numbers of professional doctorate programmes during the early years of the twenty-first century in the UK is an example of how reflective practice has entered the curriculum at the highest levels.

This is particularly true in those academic disciplines most closely related to higher professional learning such as nursing, education and applied social studies where Schön's notion of the 'reflective practitioner' has been influential (Schön, 1983) in the development of professionalism. The work of educational development units in HE institutions also expanded rapidly over the last decade of the twentieth century (Gosling, 2001) encouraging reflective learning among lecturing staff through staff development courses. A survey of the promotional literature on these courses suggested that the conceptual underpinnings were dominated by two ideas: 1) Kolb's experiential learning cycle, and 2) Schön's reflective practitioner (Bourner, France and Atkinson, 2000) with reflective learning playing a key role in both ideas. These courses are intended to prepare and develop teachers from across the spectrum of the subject disciplines of HE and in so doing they bring the concept of reflective learning into every part of the academy.

Students need to be guided on how to write reflectively and given permission to use the first person in assessed work. Writing about personal experience does not come easily to students from the humanities and social sciences, who for years have been trained to write only in the third person, in order to encourage objectivity. However, for students from the hard sciences, including, for example, engineering, product design or mathematics, who are only occasionally required to write at all, it presents a different kind of challenge. The requirement to keep a weekly log is a valuable discipline in tracking a personal development journey but a huge culture shift for those who are used to worrying about their assignments at the last minute and who are not in the habit of producing material on a weekly basis that contributes to a final piece of work.

Approaches to encourage reflective writing have included:

- an initial group exercise which requires students to
  identify an event, describe it in a group, then analyse it,

172

reflect on it, and discuss the difference between the three accounts;

- using a structured notebook that has to be filled in at different points in an experiential project (on preparing for an interview, in going to a first meeting, three weeks into the project, mid-way through the project, at the end of the project and three weeks after finishing);
- posting reflections online at particular intervals or stages in their work;
- encouraging students to apply the questions to guide reflective thinking on pages 77–78; and
- being given free rein to write in whatever way worked best for them, and as freely as possible providing they captured the feelings associated with the experience. This might include writing in a notebook on the bus on the way home, typing thoughts onto a computer document and recording the experience on a mobile phone.

None of these approaches are problem-free. Regardless of any emphasis placed on the importance of tracking a journey, there are still those who mock up logs in the week before an assessment is due, taking the trouble to write in different coloured pens to simulate a document that had been compiled over many weeks. However, thinking back to 'how you felt' at the start of an event is never the same as recording feelings as they are experienced and without the value of hindsight.

Moon (2004) draws attention to the different levels of reflection and provides exercises that included a series of accounts of a single event which illustrate increasingly deep levels of reflection. Her resources are valuable in helping students to identify the difference between the accounts and the additional learning that comes from reflecting during and at a distance from a single event.

Other approaches include using:

- a mirror (analysing yourself as you might be viewed through someone else's eyes);
- a microscope (analysing a detail from an experience – possibly one that went well and one that went badly) and using it as a critical incident to illustrate something about the experience as a whole, making the small large; and

- binoculars (seeing an object in the distance and viewing an experience within a broader contextual landscape).

Developing students' capacity for reflective learning is part of developing their capacity to learn how to learn but unless done well and with proper commitment to learning, their value is limited. Putting aside a seminar to look into different approaches to reflection and journal writing is probably time well spent. See also www.artofmanliness. com/2009/06/07/30-days-to-a-better-man-day-8-start-a-journal/ and www.theguardian.com/news/oliver-burkemans-blog/2013/jul/18/ why-keeping-a-journal

Creating legitimate assessment processes

If SCE is to become a legitimate part of most HE programmes, course leaders need to be clear about their ability to assess it accurately and fairly and to a standard commensurate with the other modules on a course of learning. The framework developed by Owen and Hill was based on an extensive literature review on policies and practices associated with SCE and on a previously developed 'Framework for attributes' for engaging with the public and is suggested as a guide for thinking through how to approach assessment design.

A key part of all SCE work is the ability to use reflection effectively and many of the other attributes for engagement are also assessed through different forms of reflective learning and the production of reflective documents, whether as reports, structured logs, blogs or video diaries. However, a significant and variable proportion of reflective learning outcomes are *subjective* knowledge rather than *objective* knowledge. Only the person doing the reflection can assess whether learning has occurred that is significant to them, while the notion of secure assessment implies some form of evaluation against an independent standard. If the rest of the world is to find the assessment useful the standard of assessment must be explicit. In the case of personal learning from SCE, it is difficult to see what external standard can be used for measuring the worth of the learning.

Assessment normally involves a judgment of the extent to which planned learning outcomes have been achieved by students. Reflection is the process of turning experience into learning and that learning is *emergent* rather than *planned*. It is difficult to specify, a priori, planned learning outcomes for a process that yields emergent learning outcomes. In the absence of planned learning outcomes there is nothing against which to assess the learning. Community development courses, management training and communications as a discipline area all have something to contribute to a theoretical understanding of SCE and provide models of assessment that might be adopted for particular tasks. The assessment of critical thinking, which has a longer history in HE, also provides some useful pointers for a way forward.

In 1991 Sir Douglas Hague, the chair of the Economic and Social Research Council for much of the 1980s, wrote of critical thinking, the ability to judge ideas and evidence,

> *Academics must believe that acquiring the ability to test ideas and evidence is the primary benefit of a university education.* (Hague, 1991, p. 64)

Identifying evidence in student work of their ability to apply critical questions to texts (see Chapter Four) provides an indication of their skill in critical thinking. It would follow, therefore, that a similar strategy could be used for reflection. The first step is to notice the difference in terminology between 'critical *thinking*' and 'reflective *learning*'. The terms 'critical learning' or 'reflective thinking' are rarely used but it might be useful to look for similarities between 'critical *thinking*' and 'reflective *thinking*'. Replacing the term 'reflective learning' with 'reflective thinking' separates out the *process* of reflection (i.e. reflective thinking) from the *content* of that thinking and it is the subjective nature of the content that is a major barrier to the assessment of reflective learning.

Simply reviewing what happened does not constitute reflective thinking, just as reviewing a book does not involve analysis. It is as possible to review an experience unreflectively as it is to read a book uncritically, and it is the interrogation of a past experience through searching questions that provides evidence of reflective thinking. Just as the process of critical thinking implies asking searching questions, so the process of reflective thinking in SCE involves interrogating an experiencing with searching questions. The different questions to be used to elicit reflective, strategic and critical thinking provided in Chapter Four of this book are useful in attempting to measure the quality of the thinking in all three of these areas. In many SCE programmes critical, reflective and strategic thinking are all used at different points in a project process. These question frameworks could be valuable in making clear the different approaches and assessing the quality of the thinking in different elements of the programme.

Although the *content* of reflective learning in SCE may be subjective the *process* of reflective learning is not. This is because 1) the core of the reflective learning process is interrogating experience with searching questions, and 2) searching questions can be identified independently of the content of the reflection. Reflective learning is not what happens to a student, it is what the student does with what has happened, and in assessing reflection it is important not to just assess the content of an experience but rather what a student has done with the content.

There is a parallel here with project work where students select the content of their own projects but are assessed on common learning outcomes. What is measured is the *processes* employed in undertaking the project as evidenced in project reports rather than the project content. Similarly in SCE there is less concern with the content of an experience other than how the student processes it. Although the content of a student's experience may be subjective the process of reflective thinking is not. It is worth keeping in mind the implications of this for community partners who may be less concerned with the process of a student's reflective thinking and more with the impact they are able to make in the context in which they are engaged.

The other main problem in assessing reflective learning from SCE is that learning outcomes can only be determined *after* the process. This is a problem insofar as assessment is viewed as forming a judgment about whether the *prior* learning outcomes of a course of study have been achieved. This becomes more difficult when assessing the *process* of reflective learning from SCE and it is important to separate the process (i.e. reflective thinking) from the content (i.e. the experience itself). Once the content/process distinction has been made, it becomes possible to specify a learning outcome in advance in terms of one relating to the capacity for reflective thinking. The intended learning outcome could then be phrased in terms of 'the capacity to think reflectively' or, less abstractly, 'the capacity to capture the lessons of experience'.

Critical thinking and reflective thinking from SCE share a common two-stage structure:

1. Bringing material into conscious awareness.
2. Asking and responding to searching questions.

In the case of critical thinking the first stage is achieved by such means as reading a book or listening to a lecture; the second stage is achieved through what the student does with the content of the book or the lecture. In the case of reflective learning from SCE, the first stage is achieved by reviewing a past experience to recall it as vividly and comprehensively as possible; the second stage is achieved through what the student does with what has been recalled.

The literature on students' orientations to study often makes the distinction between 'deep' and 'surface' learning (Entwistle, 2001). Surface learning is associated with uncritical accumulation of facts and opinions, whereas deep learning is associated with critical thinking. Surface learners, like uncritical thinkers, read a book without asking the sort of searching questions of it that enable them to create their own meanings from the text; they take it in at face value. By contrast, deep learners, like critical thinkers, read in a questioning way. Deep learners, like critical thinkers, find more in what they read because they ask searching questions of it.

Within the domain of reflective learning from SCE, the distinction between surface learning and deep learning is equally applicable. In this domain, surface learning is associated with unreflective thinking and deep learning is associated with reflective thinking. Surface learners are those who can describe their experience but do not ask searching questions of it; they simply take it at face value. Deep learners, by contrast, engage with their experience in a questioning way. In the domain of reflective learning from SCE, deep learners, like reflective thinkers, get more from their experience because they ask searching questions of it. The distinction between passive learning and active learning is also applicable to reflective learning from SCE: experience is what happens to a student, reflective thinking is what the student does with what happens to them.

This suggests that one reason why some people are poor at reflective learning is that they have a limited repertoire of searching reflective questions. It further suggests that the key to developing reflective learners is developing such a repertoire of reflective questions and providing opportunities to practice using them. This means that student learning from community engagement can play a key role within the academy in developing the capacity for reflective learning, which is increasingly being valued as an academic approach in its own right as well as its contribution to lifelong learning.

A university education is often seen as 'developing the powers of the mind'. Sometimes this term has been construed quite narrowly as developing the power to test ideas, assertions and evidence, i.e. critical thinking. Increasingly, universities and other institutions of HE see the need to construe the term more broadly and prepare students for lifelong learning that will comprise reflective learning as well as planned learning, and strategic and reflective as well as critical thinking. Developing a secure means of assessing reflective learning is an essential pre-requisite for this. By putting the assessment of reflective thinking about SCE on the same footing as the assessment of critical thinking, this chapter contributes to that outcome. It offers a secure method of assessing reflective learning, which is a core learning outcome of any course of SCE.

References

Boud, D., Keogh, R. and Walker, D. (eds) (1985) *Reflection: Turning Experience into Learning*. London: Kogan Page.

Bourner, T., France, L. and Atkinson, A. (2000) *Preparing and Developing University Teachers: An Empirical Study*. Education Research Centre Occasional Paper, University of Brighton.

Brennan, J. and Little, B. (1996) *A Review of Work Based Learning in Higher Education*. London: Department for Education and Employment.

Entwistle, N. (2001) 'Styles of learning and approaches to studying in higher education', *Kybernetes* 30(5/6), pp. 593–603.

Gosling, D. (2001) 'Educational development units in the UK – what are they doing five years on?', *The International Journal for Academic Development*, 6(1), pp. 74–90.

Hague, D. (1991) *Beyond Universities: A New Republic of the Intellect*. Hobart Paper 115. London: Institute of Economic Affairs.

Matthews, B. (2006) *Engaging Education: Developing Emotional Literacy, Equity and Co-education*. Buckingham: McGraw-Hill/Open University Press.

Matthews, B. and Snowden, E. (2007) *Making Science Lessons Engaging, More Popular, and Equitable Through Emotional Literacy*. London: Goldsmiths College. At: http://eprints.gold.ac.uk/3599/1/matthews-emotional_literacy.pdf [accessed December 2013].

Moon, J. (2004) *A Handbook of Reflective and Experiential Learning, Theory and Practice*. Abingdon: RoutledgeFarmer.

Owen, D. (2012) *Community Based Learning, Experiences from the University of Bristol*, NCCPE. At: www.hestem-sw.org.uk/project?id=38&pp=553 [accessed March 2014].

QUAAHE (1998) *A Consultation Paper on Qualifications Frameworks: Postgraduate Qualifications*. London: The Quality Assurance Agency for Higher Education.

Schön, D (1983) *The Reflective Practitioner*. San Francisco: Jossey Bass.

Weare, K. (2003) *Developing the Emotionally Literate School*. London: Paul Chapman.

Section Three

Reflecting on Student–Community Engagement

CHAPTER NINE

Evaluating and embedding student–community engagement

With contributions from Simon Northmore

Introduction

This chapter examines ways in which community-engaged programmes might best be evaluated and who should be involved in the design of the evaluation process. It discusses the additional challenges involved in the proper evaluation of SCE when compared to more traditional approaches to teaching and learning and the benefits of using broader evaluation methodologies. Drawing on experiences from the University of Brighton's Community–University Partnership Programme (CUPP), which has been developing its work in evaluating community-engaged courses since 2003, this chapter aims to provide some practical ideas for developing a systematic evaluation approach. It suggests that by looking closely at the purposes of SCE and how this is shared by different stakeholders, having a sense of key learning for both students and stakeholders and the benefits of community projects, will assist in embedding SCE more effectively in the curriculum.

Putting evaluation in context

The claims made by programmes of learning from community engagement are that they provide 'added value' to higher education for students, increase students' sense of social responsibility, and form part of the wider social mission of the modern university.

For students, this additionality includes claims made for: a broadening of horizons and sense of social concern; a locus for the practical application of their academic studies; enhanced employability, academic performance and interpersonal skills; and greater self-knowledge and capacity for reflective thinking (Millican and Bourner, 2011). An extensive literature review from the USA (Eyler *et al.*, 2001) summarises research into the impacts of service learning over a period of seven years. The research cites improvements in areas as diverse as students' academic attainment while still at university, career development on leaving university, and social commitment and involvement throughout their future lives. While much of this literature is now more than ten years old, stemming from the resurgence of service learning in the 1990s, it does indicate that well-organised programmes can have significant benefits for students, institutions and communities.

However, these claims are not only wide ranging but also reflect a tension between academic, citizenship and employability outcomes. Most evaluation has focused on outcomes for students, while very little is focused on community partners and the broader contributions to the university. Stoecker and Tyron explore the lack of a community response in *Unheard Voices* (2007) but are almost a lone voice in including this perspective. These tensions provide an important context in which to think about the questions to ask in the evaluation of SCE and the people to approach.

There are increased, and accelerating, expectations on HE to develop graduates who are both socially responsible and able to work in a multifaceted, competitive knowledge environment. SCE makes claims to deliver on both those things, which are often in tension with each other. Expectations of social responsibility include the notion of gifting time, a commitment to exploring inequalities and values and question-ing injustices, from the position of the university as a public institution. Employability agendas are more compatible with privatised notions of a university, seeing a degree as a route to personal future wealth and encouraging students to seek out opportunities that will benefit their own futures. A successful citizenship-orientated programme might measure changes in the values and attitudes of students and their involve-ment in local communities. An employment-orientated programme might be more concerned with the development of skills, the work readiness of graduates and the speed in which they move into future careers. Any move to institutionalise and embed an SCE programme is likely to encounter opposing attitudes to the core purpose of a university and the extent to which staff should involve themselves in these different areas of a student's future. Similarly, moves to embed a programme strategically across an institution invariably lead to it being used and interpreted differently, across schools and faculties. This lack of clarity about the purpose of engagement lies behind the challenges involved in evaluation in this arena; it is difficult to evaluate the impact of a programme without being clear about its purpose.

Approaches to evaluation

A literature review undertaken at the University of Brighton listed three current problems with measuring university–community engagement: a lack of focus on outcomes, a lack of standardised instruments and tools, and the variety of approaches currently being adopted. The subsequent briefing paper prepared for the NCCPE on public engagement auditing, benchmarking, and evaluating (Hart, Northmore and Gerhardt, 2009) concluded that measurement approaches that include economic dimensions and impacts on community well-being 'merit further development ... if we are to successfully demonstrate the worth of public engagement.' (p. 39). While a number of tools have been developed that aim to capture the impact of community–university partnerships, and there are a range of auditing and benchmarking frameworks concerned with outcomes for a university, there have been few attempts at producing evaluation frameworks that focus on community perspectives.

For example, the Carnegie Foundation's *Elective Classification for Community Engagement* from the USA (http://classifications. carnegiefoundation.org) provides a useful set of detailed indicators for curricular engagement, outreach and partnership but fails to include responses from community partners. The classification process gathers evidence-based documentation of institutional practice as part of a process of self-assessment and quality improvement.

Community engagement involves collaborating between institutions of HE and their larger communities (local, regional/state, national, global) for the mutually beneficial exchange of knowledge and resources in a context of partnership and reciprocity. The purpose of community engagement is the partnership of college and university knowledge and resources with those of the public and private sectors to enrich scholarship, research, and creative activity; enhance curriculum, teaching and learning; prepare educated, engaged citizens; strengthen democratic values and civic responsibility; address critical societal issues; and contribute to the public good. (http://classifications.carnegiefoundation. org/descriptions/community_engagement.php).

Despite this, as an institutional classification rather than an evaluation tool, the documentation is not so useful for capturing data on activities that are intended primarily to have a social impact. The university reapplies for classification every five years in order to maintain an institutional quality mark and the institution is rated on how it views engagement and how far it is able to mediate and share knowledge:

> *Community engagement describes activities that are undertaken with community members. In reciprocal partnerships, there are collaborative community-campus definitions of problems, solutions, and measures of success. Community engagement requires processes in which academics recognize, respect, and value the knowledge, perspectives, and resources of community partners and that are designed to serve a public purpose, building the capacity individuals, groups, and organizations involved to understand and collaboratively address issues of public concern.* (Taken from First Time Classification Documentation Framework: http://classifications.carnegiefoundation.org/ downloads/community_eng/first-time_framework.pdf)

Attempts to measure levels of community engagement at the University of Brighton began with an audit carried out at the university in order to create a benchmark against which to measure future change. In a bold move to embed community engagement into the University's Corporate Plan 2007–12 it set itself a specific target, to carry out 'a baseline and subsequent audit of community engagement in which the data show increased levels of engagement and local benefit from university activities' (University of Brighton, 2007).

The audit threw up the range of engagement activities across the institution and claimed a 90 per cent response rate, but struggled with the demarcation between the engaged activities of an institution and the volunteering of individuals undertaken in their own time. It excluded events that were primarily about promoting individual access to the University, or the result of hosting publicly-accessible facilities, and aimed to focus on mutually beneficial activities that were linked to the University's core tasks of teaching and research. It highlighted, *the extent to which engagement activities have a real relationship with teaching, learning and research at the University: this is not a bolt-on extra. One example is the 36 modules taught in the University to over 950 students and the 12,000 student hours spent on placements. And this does not include courses in teaching education or nursing where students are by definition learning in the professional communities in which they will subsequently practice. A second example is the 72 research projects involving community partnerships, of which 11 originated in an enquiry from the community itself* (University of Brighton, 2008)

Moves to repeat a University-wide audit in 2012 were hampered by the difficulty of gathering accurate data from across the University and the lack of a means to collate and compare this. The group tasked with this activity concluded that celebrating achievement by providing a facility for faculty to self-publicise engaged work was a better use of time and resources than attempting to track and measure the diversity of activities across a large institution. As a result, CUPP published a series of case studies in 2013 (University of Brighton, 2013a) and the University is currently developing a web-based mapping tool to record case studies of engaged practice across the city in a way that both community and University participants can contribute to.

Another approach tried in Brighton was using the REAP framework, developed at the University of Bradford (Pearce and Pearson, 2007). This was designed to measure and evaluate community engagement against four overarching principles: reciprocity, externalities, access and partnerships. Reciprocity here refers to the two way flow of information between communities and universities, and externalities to the benefits of engagement that extend beyond partnership participants to the broader societal or community context. However, researchers involved in its development acknowledged that measuring the broader impact of engagement outside of partnerships is very difficult and would require significant investment by institutions and local organisations in data collection. This substantiates the view of Hart, Northmore and Gerhardt (2009) that 'long-term timescales are required for measuring both higher- level institutional outcomes and broader social/community outcomes' (p. 11).

Langworthy, from Swinburne University, who has written extensively on the Australian Universities Community Engagement Alliance

(AUCEA) benchmarking pilot project in Australia, notes that approaches to measuring community engagement often focus on the process of engagement rather than outcomes because of the necessity to collect longitudinal data for the latter, concluding, 'In an age of accountability and short political timelines, it is easy to be seduced by the easily measured. But are these measures an indication of what really matters and is the process enabling universities to improve and progress?' (Langworthy, 2008, p. 1). Similarly, Hart, Northmore and Gerhardt (2009) suggest that it is more important to consider the changes brought about through engagement activities than to count the number of activities themselves.

The challenges of evaluating student–community engagement

Systematic evaluations of the difference SCE can make at community level are also few and far between. Audit approaches similarly include quantitative measures such as numbers of students involved in a community, the number of hours worked and a corresponding financial value attached to these without a real understanding of the cumulative contribution they might have made. How far these activities attract formal credit or recognition and how widely they are adopted across a university tends to be used as a measure of the institution's commitment to SCE without any strong evaluation of their impact on the culture of the university or its faculty members.

In the UK *The Volunteering Impact Assessment Framework* (Davis Smith *et al.*, 2004) a matrix for assessing the impact of volunteering published by the Institute for Volunteering Research provides a starting point for considering how to measure the impact of student involvement. It is designed for use by volunteers, organisations, users and the community, and identifies impact in relation to physical, human, economic, social and cultural capital. But it has limitations as a volunteering-focused tool and does not incorporate the specific characteristics of experiential learning and curricular engagement that is central to SCE. Unlike volunteering or community outreach programmes, SCE is a form of educational experience in which community activity is connected to an accredited academic course with testable learning outcomes. A viable evaluation framework needs to bring these two areas together in determining how far the programme has met its objectives and to evaluate impact on student, faculty and community learning and change.

Typically, evaluation involves end-of-semester or end-of-module assessment (Gallini and Moely, 2003), with all the limitations of student self-reporting that such satisfaction surveys entail. But this is limited when investigating a deeper reflective course, where students may not realise how much they have learned until some time after the immediate experience. Community engagement can also be uncomfortable and difficult for students while they are immersed in the experience but have huge value retrospectively. Survey methods with more complex questions and undertaken a semester after the module ends is a possible approach. Some of the more extensive US research into changing student attitudes (Laird, 2008) have been based on the results of pre- and post-module questionnaires, and in the USA it seems that survey research is 'the methodology of choice in service learning inquiry' (Marichal, 2010, pp. 145). Likewise, the course- or subject-specific nature of much SCE activity lends itself well to case study approaches (for example, see the wealth of material available on the National Service Learning Clearing House website, www.servicelearning.org).

Despite extensive research in the USA and the value of survey and case study approaches, the overall impression is that evaluative research of the broader impacts in this field is partial and inconclusive. Samples in the UK are often small and evaluations rarely randomly assign students involved in the studies. Much research fails to clearly define and measure outcomes (Eyler, 2002). There has been little longitudinal research or comparative research into programmes at different institutions, which would test the generalisability of these claims (Gallini and Moely, 2003). It has therefore proved difficult to implement the feedback gained or use it systematically for programme improvement (Bringle and Hatcher, 2009). In addition, Bringle and Hatcher, reviewing the first wave of submissions to the Carnegie Foundation's Elective Classification for Community Engagement, 'found little evidence of community impact through service learning courses' (2009, p. 43) and a lack of community input in the submissions. Given the different levels at which SCE operates and the multiple relationships involved, this may be unsurprising. Nonetheless, as a central element of community–university partnership activity in many universities, and of growing importance in UK programmes, effective evaluation of SCE should incorporate its impact on students, faculty members, institutions and communities.

A further challenge of evaluation is the diversity of forms that SCE can take, ranging from being an integral part of professional training to an 'add-on' option as part of a modular degree programme or a general volunteering option. Often such programmes are subject or course specific and may be as varied, for example, as an SCE programme in Spanish, where students learning Spanish volunteered in local Spanish-speaking communities (Morris, 2001), or engagement tailored to the needs of graduate public administration students (Reinke, 2003). Finding reliable criteria that can take account of all of these areas remains difficult.

The expansion in service learning courses and other engaged campus–community models since the 1990s has led to an increase in empirical studies of such courses on student outcomes in terms of academic engagement and university retention (Gallini and Moely, 2003). However, as Eyler observed in 2002, 'there has been little study of the impact of service-learning on communities and on institutional goals' (Eyler, 2002, p. 518). Neither have many systematic studies emerged in the ten or so years since then, largely due to the difficulties in gathering institutional and community data. More recently, Metzger observed the lack of data on 'the other "learner" in the whole process … the faculty member' (Metzger, 2012, p. 108), which has also received little attention in evaluations of SCE.

One focus of evaluation has been on academic engagement and retention. Gallini and Moely (2003) cite several studies indicating that students evaluating service-learning courses were more likely to report that their courses promoted interpersonal, community and academic engagement than students evaluating other types of courses. This was positively associated with student satisfaction and retention. In their own study, Gallini and Moely found that it was the academic challenge of service learning courses that most influenced retention, in particular the opportunity for students to apply and reflect on the concepts they were learning in 'real world' situations and the relevance of these to their broader academic programmes.

Eyler's (2002) review of research on service learning indicates that courses which integrate academic and service learning are the most effective in developing the knowledge, skills and attributes important for civic engagement. There is also evidence that involvement in service learning programmes is a predictor of future community involvement in adult life. However, she emphasises the importance of intentional efforts to make reflection part of the process, both before, during and after the project or placement. This is critical to success: 'Just adding a service project or placement to a course does not guarantee that students will reflect on ways that the experience relates to their academic study' (2002, pp. 522–3).

In their study of a service learning course, Simons and Clearly suggest that, for the majority of students, it is social-emotional learning – 'the process through which people learn to recognise and manage emotions, care about others, and make responsible decisions to solve problems' (2006, p. 317) built through their relationship with community members – that underpins the academic learning, personal and social outcomes of service learning. Simons and Cleary caution that 'research on service learning and outcomes is mixed' (2006, p. 308), highlighting many of the methodological problems already discussed. Nonetheless, despite its acknowledged limitations, there is an accumulation of evidence for the academic, social and personal benefits of community engaged courses for students.

The notable missing area in research into SCE is the community benefit of such engagement. There is little in the literature on civic engagement and service learning which documents the community perspective (McIlrath, 2012) and little evidence of the impact of engagement on local communities. Stoecker et al. (2010) demonstrate through their conversations with community partners that service learning often places the needs and requirements of the faculty members and students first, with community organisations merely serving as the backdrop for learning. The result very often is an absence of community 'voice' and no genuine engagement at institutional level.

'A Framework for the Assessment of Student Learning from Public Engagement' (Owen and Hill, 2011, see Chapter Eight of this book, section 'Developing an assessment framework') incorporates the co-creation of knowledge between students and communities and provides clear assessment criteria against measurable outcomes. It is not unfathomable that elements of this could be adapted for future evaluations.

Different approaches used at the University of Brighton

Evaluative research needs to be context driven. What works well in one situation may not be appropriate in another. As a case study the experience of the University of Brighton, rather than offering a definitive approach, sets out to examine how context determines the questions asked and the approaches used. The study also reflects many of the limitations illustrating some of the issues discussed in the sections above, and the areas that need to be improved on in the future.

At Brighton, SCE started with a cross-university generic module provided by CUPP, offering accredited community-based work through a series of essays and reflective assignments. As it has developed, CUPP has provided support to schools to develop new modules and include community engagement in existing modules. The various SCE programmes, although varying in their nature and take-up, now operate in all schools within the university and broadly fit with CUPP's philosophy of mutual benefit and knowledge exchange. They thus differ from work placements (where students are often passive observers of a role they hope to move into in the future) and volunteering programmes. Student community research (SCR) now forms an additional element of the SCE programme, working with postgraduate students who are able to attract the support of an academic supervisor to oversee a community-based research project.

The context for these developments has been the University's decision in 2006 to commit it to 'becoming recognised as a leading UK university for the quality and range of its work in economic and social engagement and productive partnerships' (University of Brighton, 2007, p. 14). Equal emphasis was placed on social and economic engagement, with the intention that social engagement work should be for the mutual benefit of community partners and the quality of education and research that the University was able to offer. In its Social Engagement Strategy (University of Brighton, 2009) the goals of social engagement and employability are not seen as in opposition but, rather, the application of principles of social engagement to learning and teaching is seen as enhancing both the quality of the student experience and the skills employers want to see.

The University's new Strategic Plan 2012–15 (University of Brighton, 2012) takes further the commitment to embedding economic and social engagement within the undergraduate curriculum, promising a 'transformational learning experience…' (p. 8) and committing the University to the undertaking that 'All undergraduate courses will offer, as part of the curriculum, the opportunity for external engagement' (p. 15). The intention was to provide every Brighton undergraduate student with the opportunity to have at least 10 credits of their degree award linked to community-based learning or entrepreneurship by 2015. A cross-university audit of the undergraduate programmes offered found that already to be the case although take up was patchy and varied considerably.

In its policy statements the University of Brighton has consistently linked citizenship, social justice and sustainability aims with employability and market outcomes. As Millican (2013) points out, how far these competing discourses of citizenship and employability constitute a problem for the University and the students it attracts has yet to emerge. However, from the point of view of evaluating its SCE programme, it underscores the further challenge of ensuring that evaluations are sufficiently broad in scope and able to validate activity against all of these different priorities.

To this end, CUPP has adopted a mixed-method approach to evaluating student engagement but this process is still in its early stages and its limitations are apparent. Until recently CUPP, like many other institutions, tended to rely on conventional end of module evaluations and focused more on instrumental concerns such as the student experience and employability, rather than on outcomes for local communities and organisations. Efforts to address this in recent years have included the development of focus groups with students, email surveys with community partners, case study approaches of particular student projects, tutor forums, and a small-scale research study.

Student focus groups

In 2012–13 focus group interviews with students were led by a third-year Hastings undergraduate student and a Master's student. The intention behind this was that student-led discussion would yield more in terms of learning than end-of-course evaluations. One set of focus groups with social science students looked both at how students understood the module, how they valued the experience, and the difficulties encountered in terms of teaching and assessment. The latter brought out some specific issues in relation to changes in module management in that particular year, but there were some broader conclusions associated with engaged modules. There was a strong consensus on the benefits of the module in the experience it gave students of working in a challenging work environment and assessing their career aspirations. Additionally, some students expressed the value of the module in terms of being able to give their time and skills back to the community.

Interestingly, the second focus group, which took place at a later stage in the module, placed less emphasis than the first on their grades and more on learning from the experience and the opportunity for community engagement. The researcher suggested that when interviewing the first set of students the majority had not started their placements, while in the second focus group 'the majority of participants were far more satisfied with the module overall as their placement experience … had commenced and all the participants had a better appreciation of the other aspects of the module' (Pope, 2013).

The final research report suggested that students who found it difficult to engage with the module looked at it in employability terms, but those that managed to find relevant projects with community groups (which by the end of the year was the majority) became more interested in the complexities of community engagement and what they could personally contribute.

Community partner survey

CUPP has been gathering data from community partners annually since 2008, in order to address the absence of community perspectives in evaluation of SCE noted earlier. This has been mostly conducted by email. For a number of years now, partners involved with postgraduate projects and a selection of organisations offering undergraduate place-ments have been asked for feedback on their experience of working with students. Overwhelmingly respondents comment on the positive impact made by students both to their organisations and the individuals they work with. Sections from some of these responses are included in Chapter Eleven of this book: 'The Community Voice'. Occasionally, where there has been a problem with a student project, this follow-up has been welcomed as a means of surfacing and discussing difficulties that have arisen during the year but discussions focus on what happened and what might have happened differently. Experience seems to indicate that a more systematic evaluation of community partner experiences, with a focus on impact and outcomes for community groups as well as the learning of students, partners and faculty, would be valuable.

Case studies

In the last year, CUPP has also published a series of case studies of community–university engagement work (University of Brighton, 2013a) in an attempt to celebrate rather than to accurately measure its engagement work (see Chapter Eleven). This included two case studies written by former students of the University of Brighton and two by community partner organisations. These case studies provided an important way of celebrating and sharing work among academics and community groups, but they are also useful in enabling us to capture significant data about the impact of SCE.

Kerry Dowding made the transition from student to a professional career in the third sector through the Postgraduate Certificate in Community Enterprise, working with Grassroots Suicide Prevention. She writes:

> *During my time with Grassroots I worked on three main projects: the redesign of course evaluation forms; reaching a higher quality standard of monitoring and evaluation; and qualitative research into how a mental health awareness course de-stigmatised mental health issues … The benefits have been huge for both of us. For someone like me, who wanted to follow a not-for-profit route for their career, this course was the perfect option. Having a safe space to develop skills is vital … between Grassroots and the university I felt able to make the transition from a student to professional person.*

Following her placement, Kerry continued with Grassroots as the youngest trustee of their newly formed charity.

Martin Clayton was a business student at the University. It was his experience of working within the Students' Union and the University's community engagement module that combined to give him the skills to move into a community-focused career. Martin says:

> *Splitting my final year into two part-time years (due to working in a full time position within the Students' Union) I took advantage of a module outside the Business School… the community engagement module run by the university's Community University Partnership Programme.*

> *Students undertake practical projects with local community and voluntary organisations. It gave me an understanding of the theories and principles that, unbeknown to me, were influencing my SU work all the time. I was able to critique social and community theories and analyse organisational models. This allowed me to approach partner organisations appropriately in order to represent students effectively.*

Martin went on to work for Lewes Community Football Club, a cooperative football club run and entirely owned by the local community.

Research study

During the academic year 2012–13 a small-scale research study was undertaken at the University of Brighton focusing on the expectations and priorities of undergraduate students entering the University and how it could work with them most effectively to create civically engaged scholars. Through exploring student expectations of the University and of their degree and their attitudes towards civic responsibility, it set out to examine the tensions between students as 'consumers' (prioritising future employment and personal gain) and students as 'citizens' (prioritising civic involvement and social justice). By investigating these priorities the study would help inform the ways in which we could best work with students to deliver an engaged, value-based curriculum.

The detailed results of this study are available elsewhere (Millican, 2014). Of note, however, is that while community engagement as a term was not really understood, most students said that experience 'in the real world' was important, not just 'to go on the CV' but also for their learning. As one put it, 'to learn about equalities and disabilities and human rights, as there are not many places you can go to, to learn things like that'. The research demonstrated students' awareness of the value a university brought to its community, of how students bring income into the area, their potential role as volunteers with local community groups, and the value of academics researching local issues.

While these initiatives are limited in scope, they confirm the value of a broad-based approach to evaluation that is university wide rather than limited to individual modules or courses. As the role of CUPP changes from one of developing and managing student engagement to a more strategic role in supporting pedagogical approaches and coordinating relationships with community partners, its role in developing systematic evaluation (including student learning, staff learning, organisational learning and community outcomes) will become increasingly important.

Embedding in institutional structures

Upscaling or institutionalising a programme brings challenges as well as advantages. While the inclusion of SCE in an organisation's strategic mission legitimises it and provides a mechanism for developing modules across different schools and faculties, as these are pushed out to be delivered by new course teams they are in danger of losing their reciprocal nature and their focus on social justice. Like any upscaled programme, as elements of it are taken forward in different ways they can quickly become watered down versions of work experience without a sense of value or purpose. For example, institutionalising SCE presents opportunities to include SCE as an essential element of all newly validated modules and to embed it in course approval programmes. Such approaches, like insisting on the inclusion of sustainability in all course outlines, can reduce it to a tick list response on the part of course developers, who address it because they are compelled to without any real understanding of its purposes or advantages. It also raises the question as to whether these are best delivered by 'engagement professionals' who have experience of voluntary sector partnerships, or discipline specialists who are familiar with the culture of the school in which they are based and will already have community contacts within their field of work.

Ten years into the CUPP programme, as the offer for engaged opportunities has become part of the university's commitment to its students and its mission in terms of its local community, it has begun to seem as if the only way forward is to devolve the leadership of SCE modules to the schools in which they are based. The impossibility of running modules for 3000 students suggests it is time to consider a quality assurance rather than an operational role in relation to SCE work. As a result CUPP has begun to work responsively, supporting faculty members to take on leadership of SCE modules and locating the brokering of community projects within the volunteering team. This frees up time to focus on working in new schools to develop additional modules with them, adapting learning outcomes to fit the requirements of the discipline area.

It also opens up scope for cross-university pedagogic support. This is now offered through:

- seminars on SCE as part of the Postgraduate Certificate in Academic Practice, undertaken by all new members of academic staff joining the university;
- an annual cross-university symposium to which all leaders of engaged modules are invited, to share experience contacts and partners and to discuss academic practice;

- ongoing support for module development and availability to deliver on specific elements of new SCE programmes; and
- the design and development of an evaluation framework that can be offered for use in all schools across the university undertaking engaged work.

Pointers towards good practice

The experience of evaluating SCE at Brighton highlights many of the challenges of evaluation in this field that have been documented elsewhere. Since its inception in 2003, CUPP's approach to social engagement has been one of experiment or 'defining in the doing', as it is sometimes described (University of Brighton, 2013b). However, recent developments in our approach to evaluating student engagement have been indicative of a conscious attempt to develop a more disciplined approach. In the process we have learnt much and had the opportunity to assess some of the key areas we need to clarify.

Some of the questions that seem to be important in evaluating SCE are:

- Is the intention to capture change over time or assess an individual course or module?
- If the ultimate aim is to measure impact and change, what timescales are appropriate?
- Whose perspectives are we trying to include: students, community partners, faculty members, or the institution?
- Why is it important to measure engagement from a community perspective?
- Is it important to understand how collaboration is working at an individual project or faculty member level?
- How do we help busy community partners and colleagues to understand the importance of collecting meaningful data?
- Do we need to establish targets and measure whether they have been achieved? This is likely to be important if the institution has strategic goals it wishes to achieve.

It is the answers to these questions that will shape the kind of evaluation that is undertaken and the tools that are most appropriate.

The experience at Brighton and the wider literature on SCE warn of the dangers of instrumentalism. Nonetheless, recent research suggests that students are concerned with more than 'a good degree and a job'. They are also concerned with meaningful work and making a difference in their local communities. Furthermore, these aspirations can be strengthened through practice experience.

It is not the purpose of this chapter to recommend specific tools or methods and given the diversity of activities involved precise methods are likely to be context driven. However, in order to resist the current emphasis on employability and seek to provide a more transformational experience for students, one that retains an ethos of personal development and social purpose, a more systematic approach to evaluation is crucial. Yet, while some of these less tangible aspects of SCE are undoubtedly difficult to measure, rigorously incorporating student, community and faculty perspectives is a start to this process. At Brighton there is still some way to go in achieving this but by sharing experience and reflections the development of reliable approaches to evaluation can become part of a shared, inter-university enterprise.

References

Astin, A.W. and Vogelgesang, L.J. (2000) 'Comparing the effects of community service and service learning', *Michigan Journal of Community Service Learning*, 7, pp. 25–34.

Bringle, R.G. and Hatcher, J.A. (2009) 'Innovative practices in service learning and curricular engagement', *New Directions for Higher Education*, 147, pp. 37–46.

Carnegie Foundation (n.d.) *Elective Classification for Community Engagement*. At: http://classifications.carnegiefoundation.org/descriptions/community_engagement.php [accessed 5 February 2014].

Carnegie Foundation (n.d.) *First Time Classification Documentation Framework*. At: http://classifications.carnegiefoundation.org/downloads/community_eng/first-time_framework.pdf [accessed 5 February 2014].

Davis Smith, J., Gaskin, K., Ellis, A. and Howlet, S. (2004) *Volunteering Impact Assessment Toolkit. A Practical Guide for Measuring Volunteering*. London: The Institute for Volunteering Research.

Eyler, J. (2002) 'Reflection: Linking service and learning – Linking students and communities', *Journal of Social Issues*, 58(3), pp. 517–34.

Eyler, J.S., Giles, D.E., Stenson, C.M. and Gray, C.J. (2001) *At A Glance: What We Know About The Effects of Service-Learning on College Students, Faculty,*

Institutions and Communities, 1993–2000 (3rd edn). Available at: http://ewucommunityengagement.pbworks.com/w/file/fetch/62951195/aag.pdf [accessed 7 January 2014].

Gallini, S.M. and Moely, B.E. (2003) 'Service learning and engagement, academic challenge and retention', *Michigan Journal of Community Service Learning*, 10(1), pp. 5–14.

Hart, A., Northmore, S. and Gerhardt, C. (2009) *Auditing, Benchmarking, and Evaluating Public Engagement*. Bristol: National Coordinating Centre for Public Engagement.

Metzger, J. (2012) 'Teaching civic engagement', *Gateways: International Journal of Community Research and Engagement*, 5, pp. 98–114.

Millican, J. (2014) 'Engagement and employability: Student expectations of higher education', *AISHE-J, The All Ireland Journal of Teaching and Learning in Higher Education*, 6(1).

Millican, J. and Bourner, T. (2011) 'Student–community engagement and the changing role and context of higher education', *Education and Training* 53(2/3), pp. 88–99.

Morris, F.A. (2001) 'Serving the community and learning a foreign language: Evaluating a service-learning programme', *Language, Culture and Curriculum*, 14(3), pp. 244–54.

Pearce, J. and Pearson, M. (2007) *The Ivory Tower and Beyond: Bradford University at the Heart of Its Communities*. Bradford: University of Bradford.

Pope, M. (2013) 'Evaluating the Community Participation Module SS251 and examining students' engagement with the module'. University of Brighton: unpublished Master's research project report.

Reinke, S.J. (2003) 'Making a difference: Does service learning promote civic engagement in MPA students?', *Journal of Public Education* 9(2), pp. 129–38.

Simons, L. and Cleary, B. (2006) 'The Influence of Service Learning on Students' Personal and Social Development', *College Teaching, Vol. 54, No. 4, 307-319*.

Stoecker, R., Loving, K., Reddy, M. and Bollig, N. (2010) 'Can community-based research guide service learning?', *Journal of Community Practice*, 18, pp. 280–96.

University of Brighton (2007) *Corporate Plan*. Brighton: University of Brighton.

University of Brighton (2008) *University of Brighton Community Engagement Report 2006–7*. Brighton: University of Brighton.

University of Brighton (2013a) *Learning to Make a Difference: The University of Brighton and its Local Communities*. Brighton: University of Brighton Community University Partnership Programme.

University of Brighton (2013b) *Defining in the Doing*. Brighton: University of Brighton Community University Partnership Programme.

CHAPTER TEN

The student experience

Introduction

This chapter comprises a collection of narratives written by students about their experience of community engagement while studying at university. All examples have been taken from undergraduate or postgraduate students associated with the University of Brighton, although one, a Ph.D. student, studied in Barcelona before coming to Brighton as a post-doctoral research fellow. It looks at their intentions for choosing engaged modules, why they got involved in their particular project, what they gained from it, what went wrong, what they felt they were able to offer to the organisation and what they learned. The excerpts were chosen from a range emailed in response to a request for student writing covering these areas and their names are included here. The authors chose these excerpts as the most representative of issues raised at different stages of a university programme and from a range of discipline areas. By collecting them together in a single chapter it is possible to identify some key themes emerging and how these corroborate or challenge the intentions of their tutors. The chapter ends with a discussion on the value of SCE to undergraduate, postgraduate and doctoral students and their different motivations for engaging with it.

Students' motivations for engagement

Many claims have been made both earlier in this book and by academics across the world about the value of engaged approaches to learning. Marullo and Edwards (2000) use Freieran terms of 'banking education' to describe traditional, content-led or transmissional approaches to learning that focus on transferring the knowledge of the lecturer into the head of the student as swiftly as possible. They contrast this with engaged learning that they describe as holistic, embedded in real-world activity, inter-disciplinary and problem-centred. Annette (2010) talks about the 'cultivation of civic virtue through political participation, which students can experience through service learning' (p. 326). He cites the Crick report (1998) on the three key strands of citizenship education, 'social and moral responsibility, political literacy and community involvement' (p. 329) and suggests that service learning, or student community engagement, is a vehicle to develop these qualities in young adults. Bringle and Hatcher (2009) discuss the importance of a learning and reflection element in any service experience that enables students 'to gain further understanding of course content, a broader appreciation of the discipline, and an enhanced sense of personal values and civic responsibility' (Bringle and Hatcher, 1995, p. 112). They suggest that students are not only 'serving to learn' but also 'learning to serve' (2009, p. 38). Bringle and Clayton (2012) discuss what a civic-minded graduate might look like and suggests a level of active engagement and a commitment to working professionally to 'effectively address issues in society for the public good' (p. 125). In reviewing the different domains and claims made for engaged learning they suggest areas such as ability to communicate, to work with diversity, to be more self-aware, to solve problems and to be committed to active engagement in advocacy or community involvement in the future.

However, recent pressures on universities to produce graduates who are employable in fields that will allow them to pay the high fees they now accumulate has led to new discourses creeping into a field that formerly prioritised citizenship and civic virtue. Lecturers promoting engaged curricula are currently as likely to talk about 'enhancing your CV', 'gaining the skills that employers want' and 'making yourself more competitive in the jobs market' than they are to discuss active citizenship. In some cases the shift has been from a banking or transmissional approach to learning to a transactional one.

Interviews with young undergraduates at the University of Brighton during the different stages of their engaged module showed a range of intentions behind their choice to work with communities. An initial poll in a group of 150 social science students showed that only 10 per cent had chosen the module 'because it looked good on a CV', with 40 per cent choosing it 'because it's important to get a sense of the community outside of the university', 20 per cent choosing it 'because the other choice looked difficult' and 20 per cent because they were 'interested in discussing values and ideas'. When asked about their long-term priorities, 30 per cent were focused on 'getting a good job and earning lots of money', the same proportion who felt it was important to 'get a job that reflects my values and aspirations'. Students interviewed during the module described its benefits both as 'being able to give my time back to the community' and 'being able to really think about where and how I might work in the future'. Students interviewed at the end described their experience in working with partners as being one of the most valuable parts of their university education.

This indicates that while students might come to university with very little idea of what community engagement is, or how it might be relevant to them, this develops during the process of being engaged with it. While lecturers might be quick to link engagement with employability outcomes it appears from the excerpts below that it is the experience of engagement that can have a lasting impact on a student's view of the world. For undergraduates this experience can be significant in reframing their future priorities while for postgraduates it can serve as a way of confirming or focusing their practice.

Kerry writes an account of an undergraduate community engagement module, why she chose it and what she gained from it:

> Community engagement was the module I selected in second year whilst studying Criminology and Sociology. I chose to volunteer at an organisation that supports the resettlement of offenders into the community. The option to choose this organisation was implied through the university, at a placement fair. This helped many students to acquire their placements. The reason for choosing this type of placement was because of how different it would be to other ones. It was clear to me that by working with such vulnerable people, I would not only see the criminal justice system first-hand, but gain experience for the field that I would consider working in after I completed university.

> At the organisation I undertook the role of 'Community Support Volunteer', mentoring the offenders who were in prison for a short amount of time. This seemed to be an interesting role and I was

initially very excited to take it on. However, my CRB check never came through whilst doing the placement, which inhibited the work that I could do. Therefore, to gain the hours, I attended monthly meetings with all the volunteers, shadowed staff members in the prison and assisted in recruitment drives around Sussex. It was rather disappointing to not be able to resettle the ex-prisoners back into society, but I was able to see the will-power many prisoners had whilst preparing to be released from prison to make positive choices in life.

Seeing how deprived many of the prisoners were, made me want to do as much as I could for them. Before starting the placement, the mental health issues, substance misuse problems, debt and lack of education did not seem to be that significant to me. But once I began discussing these issues with the prisoners, the amount of problems they had were understood. This made the option of working in a prison or for the probation service more appealing to me, because it was clear that the prisoners were fed up of going in and out of prison and really needed a lifestyle change.

The experience of working in the community has been very valuable. At first I was nervous about working with offenders, but was soon assured by everyone that it would be fine. The prisoners sign up to working with a mentor whilst they are in the prison. This indicates that they obviously want the help. I have been trained to know relevant agencies within Sussex to refer ex-prisoners to and have learnt how to become a professional mentor. I am glad I chose to apply for this and intended to carry on working there as a volunteer. Now that I have completed my placement, I will be trained to be a full mentor. The experience I will gain from this will be very useful and I am excited to know that this is the next step.

Kerry Akast, University of Brighton

Wesley, a mature student, came to Brighton after a career in the private sector with the specific intention of retraining and found engagement a valuable way into this. He writes about his experience with the same undergraduate module:

I came to Brighton University as a 30-year-old mature student, who after a successful career in sales and business decided that I need a career change. I decided I wanted to work with disadvantaged young people in the 3rd sector and the Community Participation and Development module in year 2 of my undergraduate degree, gave me the opportunity to find a placement that would allow me to gain first-hand experience of the sector.

My favourite sociologist is Loic Wacquant and during some research for an assignment I discovered that he had carried out ethnographic research in a boxing gym, where he discovered how the sport was a great mechanism for engaging disenfranchised young people. I had heard of an amazing youth engagement project in East London, called Fight for Peace and I was fortunate enough to be accepted as a volunteer in the Career and Guidance department. My role involved me working at the academy one day a week and I was responsible for managing a caseload of young people who were not in employment, education or training. A typical day would involve conducting a group session with some young people on how to enhance their career prospects or college ambitions, followed by 1:1 mentoring sessions for more demanding cases and then a debrief of the caseload at a team meeting. I enjoyed my time at FFP so much, that after completing my mandatory 60 hours as per the module requirement, I continued to volunteer at the academy until I gained full employment 2 years later, because I knew there was so much more I could learn by continuing in the placement.

The experience was challenging, rewarding, diverse, but most importantly it gave me front line involvement of working in the 3rd sector. I discovered through this placement, how the recent recession has affected the 3rd sector, with the funding cuts causing job losses and restructuring of departments. The most important lesson I learnt from my time in this role was that working in an under-funded, understaffed, multi-agency system, creates serious issues of low morale and high tension, with many people working with minimal job security. All the uncertainty however, opened my eyes to the challenges I would face once I had graduated and allowed me to be prepared for a career in this sector. Without this experience I have no doubt, I would not have been able to achieve a job in this sector.

I managed to gain employment as a Youth Engagement Coordinator and the feedback I received from my line manager as to why I was successful, was all based upon my knowledge of the sector gained through my voluntary CPD placement. My awareness of the problems that I would face and how to overcome them was the key factor in his decision to employ me.

The job that I have now involves setting up engagement projects throughout Surrey for disenfranchised young people not in employment, education or training (NEET) and I have based my current projects on the boxing engagement philosophy of FFP and the project is proving equally as successful in Surrey as it did in London. So many young people's lives are now being enhanced as a direct result of my time spent on the CPD module.

Wesley Ankrah, University of Brighton

Reem, a third-year student, reflecting on her experience of engagement and those of her colleagues, also talks about her own growing realisation of the notion of citizenship, the role of the university in this and the danger of linking engagement too closely to employability:

I think it all started with an Alistair Ross article, 'Multiple identities and definitions of Citizenship', in that I never really thought about the definition of citizenship much before, I had always sort of thought of it in the narrow territorial sense of belonging to a state, but in thinking more about it being a marriage of rights and responsibilities and who those rights are extended to, I started thinking about it more in a sort of indignant way and being more interested in what it means to other people, active citizenship and civic engagement is something that I confess I haven't always been the most active citizen myself and the most engaged. I have been interested in politics and I will read the newspaper and get worked up but I have just sort of always been an armchair politician, like a lot of people and had a bit of a cynical attitude towards the probability that anything positive could ever get done. But then that is sort of the problem in itself. In volunteering for the CAB and in learning a bit more about the processes of how to get things done and how to affect change I think I became totally obsessed with this whole subject area.

[The article]... was introduced to me in the first year where it was one of three readings that we were discussing but [it]... was one that stayed with me and that I revisited in essays often.

[The engaged module] was compulsory. I was a bit indignant – although the lectures, looking back on them included a lot of interesting content but they were somewhat dry, we talked about the notion of graduatedness, that's one thing that really sticks out in my memory. I guess at the time the point was they wanted us to get work experience. In the first few weeks of secondary school and in the first few weeks of my GCSE year I was expected to go out and get work experience and it felt like that all over again but at university. Well the group thought of it as that, a lot of the most vocal complaints came from the more mature students who understandably felt that they were being patronised because it was being delivered for the purpose of employability more than anything else. And even among the younger students (because a lot of us have to work alongside studying to afford to be here), felt that getting work experience was not something they needed to do.

You could choose anything but it was encouraged that you worked for the voluntary sector and there was a programme that linked students to potential work experience contexts that were all in the voluntary sector and because of that people ended up in the recommended places – I am not sure whether the words 'big society' were actually said out loud but that made me feel I didn't want to be forced into voluntarism, it is something that I did anyway but I didn't like the idea of being forced into it.

I was interested in citizenship anyway but I think I was quite cross about it, and it wasn't until I later that I realised it was really about citizenship. It seemed at the time that the module being sold from an employability point of view. It was only later when I started looking at it through the lens of citizenship that I saw there was something about that they were trying to teach, I just didn't see it at the time, it just got crowded out, in order to sell it to the students.

When I asked my colleagues what they got out of the module most said work experience, one person did say that they felt it was unnecessary, but far and away the highest response was about job prospects. A lot of people said knowledge or skills for a particular type of career field, and some people said knowledge for self-growth or critical thinking, that sort of thing, but much less. Higher education is definitely seen as an investment by students and I think a lot of students do position themselves as customers.

I understand the bind that universities are in – in trying to appease the customer in a sense, because universities are more and more subject to the market and to the competitiveness they are in but I would have been a lot more brave and unapologetic about the citizenship aspect of that module and I would not bother too much as selling it as something that would improve employability. Because the whole purpose in the minds of a lot of students is to improve employability and this is one module, just one, that is for people to really think about and discuss what citizenship is about and what it means, and if it was purely focussed on this even the mature students, of which there are many would really would be much happier and people would probably contribute to the subject a lot more. There is a lot of tension between the twin aims of trying to sell citizenship as something that sells employability because at the end of the day business values tend to win out as priority.

There is a chapter in one of the books I am reading for my research and it talks about the student consumer and discusses whether it is empowering student or corroding learning. It's almost like that transactional attitude towards education they put in the money and expect a degree, and there is not so much personal input to what they are doing at university. It's like something they are expecting to receive like a product. I think that is what is sucking the passions out of students.

Reem Ibrahim, University of Brighton.

Postgraduate students, many of whom come to university with several years' experience of work, tend to have a firmer idea of future work possibilities and of what they want from a Master's programme but their work with communities can still open up future avenues for work or research. A criminology Master's student reflects on how her engaged experience led her towards a Ph.D.

During my Master's in Criminology I chose to do a course on social research practice in connection with CUPP (Community University Partnership Programme). At the time I was considering whether I should apply for a PhD to continue my studies or if I could find employment in a field related to Criminology. I knew I had enjoyed doing research during my studies and was keen to work for an organisation that was not for profit. However, I was unsure what route to follow. The course provided an opportunity to gain hands-on experience and conduct a research project for a local non-governmental organisation (NGO). Simultaneously I could increase my network of potential employers.

I was interested in examining social interventions that helped reduce crime. So I chose to conduct my research for an NGO that made promising claims of success in this field. The NGO was involved in the mentoring of ex-offenders; their aim was to enable mentees to resettle in their community and support them in maintaining their non-offending behaviour. The NGO was interested in the research as a way of obtaining evidence of their service's effectiveness in order to use this information on funding bids. They also hoped to understand whether there were areas of provision in which they needed to make changes. For these reasons, I designed a mixed-method study to evaluate the impact of the variety of activities that the organisation was involved with, while also bearing attention to numeric approaches that would be appealing to funders.

The project changed some of my ideas, insofar as I realised just how pressured NGOs are to show that they deserve funding. During the project, it became clear that their ability to achieve very complex outcomes, such as 'reducing re-offending', was very partial. I learned that individual and interpersonal approaches to reducing crime are rather limited and even though service users had benefited from mentoring, the hard data on re-offending did not show the positive results expected by the NGO. Consequently, I was faced with the dilemma of how my research would impact the organisation. Understandably, they did not publicise the report I wrote. I got a taste of how the process of doing significantly time-consuming research can be frustrating and does not always lead to predictable outcomes.

*The experience of participating in this research made me aware of
the challenges – at various dimensions, including political, individual,
discursive and epistemological – faced by charities, their clients,
their workers and those who carry out research on their behalf.
Nevertheless, the experience reinforced the feeling that I enjoyed
conducting research and I still hoped to do 'not-for-profit' work. So I
decided to apply for a Ph.D. and work towards a career in education,
where I may be able to combine research with social engagement. I
am currently a Ph.D. student at King's College London where I am
studying issues around human rights, public security and violence in
Brazil.*

Roxana Cavalcanti, University of Brighton

Another, Alison, describes her experience of running an action research
project within an arts-based MA and the opportunity it gave her to
really define her future practice:

*This project was undertaken as part of my Inclusive Arts Practice
MA. I chose to work in partnership with the Brighton Oasis Project,
focusing on Young Oasis, its service for children and young people
affected by familial substance misuse.*

*My area of interest within inclusive arts is the lack of access to the
countryside experienced by those suffering from a disability or social
exclusion. In 2003 the Countryside Agency's Diversity Review
found that while countryside activities have the potential to be
inclusive, many people currently experience real or perceived barriers
to access.*

*The methodology for this research was the act of walking in the
countryside with a group of children from Young Oasis. Together we
would explore ways to make art outdoors. I also planned a series of
indoor workshops to enable me more time to get to know the project's
young participants, aged between 5 and 14, and form an ethical
relationship based on reciprocal trust.*

*In July 2012 six children and four adults went to the Long Man of
Wilmington and enjoyed an idyllic day drawing and exploring on
the steep hillside. Organising trips into the South Downs National*

210

Park proved relatively straight-forward. The real challenge lay in spending enough time with participants: in order that Oasis child protection policies and procedures were in place, all contact had to be via the partner organisation. Thus I could see them only on weekdays (when they were at various schools across the city) or in the holidays.

In addition to the trips, I organised after-school indoor creative workshops at Oasis, but I experienced attendance problems – three consecutive sessions with no one turning up. It was soon evident that the benefits of an outdoor creative process were not in question. Rather, participants' access to many things, including the countryside, was inhibited by factors in their home lives that seemed beyond the influence of the researcher.

The Young Person's Therapist at Oasis, was able to meet frequently with me and evaluate our methods. Thus I began spending time in the Oasis office telephoning participants' parents (rather than relying on Jo to do this) in order to gain their trust, reminding them about consent forms, which were so essential to the ethical framework of the project. This approach resulted in an increase in attendance to 50% of those invited.

This was a successful partnership, based on shared aims and similar approaches, but it required time to form into a productive collaboration; time that we did not really have during a short MA research project. Time, as mentioned above, was also crucial to the ethical involvement of young vulnerable people as participants in action research.

Fortunately I was able to extend the project by two months, and by February 2013 half-term break the group had formed into an enthusiastic cohort, who expressed a keen desire to continue what we had set in motion. The fruitful partnership between the researcher and Brighton Oasis Project is something we would all like to continue, and a funding application has been made to the Edward Starr Charitable Trust with the intention of providing a programme of artwalks and trips for Young Oasis in the summer holidays.

Alison Cotton, University of Brighton

A second arts student describes the reasons behind her commitment to working on a joint research project and the ethos with which she approached her work:

> *Taking the opportunity to work with a Housing Association initially appealed to me because I have an interest in learning disability rights and social inclusion.*
>
> *My first meeting with their key point of contact, revealed that neither of us knew what was expected from this collaboration! Despite this, we were both determined to find something we could work on together, with mutual benefit. CUPP describe their key philosophy as being one of 'knowledge exchange rather than knowledge transfer', moving away from an outdated 'welfare' approach towards a more 'rights based' and actively engaged way of working with community groups (Millican et. al., 2007, p. 158). Indeed, this ethos is central to the Inclusive Arts Practice Masters and as such is at the forefront of my mind when considering projects.*

Abi Jones, University of Brighton

A postdoctoral research fellow working with us at CUPP described her experience of incorporating SCE into her Ph.D. studies. While this had been something suggested to her by her supervisor, the experience gave her a new perspective on the value of research and she went on to promote 'service learning' in her own university.

> *In 2000 I began my career in education at the University of Barcelona. My first motivation was help to dyslexic people because, I had difficulties myself in this area. During the years that I had been in University I had started to generate a new approach to learning. I questioned why pedagogy is situated almost exclusively in schools and educational institutions and began to be critical about that position, agreeing with a sentence of Paulo Freire, "No one educates anyone, and nobody is self educated; all of us learn from each other, mediated by the world we live in" (Freire, 1972). At the same time, I had the opportunity to work with Josep Ma. Puig Rovira, who spoke a different language, about the values, as well as the content, of education. When I finished my degree I had the opportunity to work*

with the United Nations Association of Spain, and in a Hospital in Barcelona. In both places I felt the need to learn more about democracy, community and education.

I signed on to a Ph.D. in "Education and Democracy", in which I had time to reflect about democracy, social education and values. During this process I learned about service-learning and ethnographic research. I went to visit an organisation working with immigrant populations. I could see how a non- educative organisation tries to effect social change through education within the social sector. This encouraged me to use the same approach within my Ph.D. working with ethnography and service learning within a non-educative organisation – The Blood and Tissue Bank of Catalonia. In my Ph.D. I wanted to know how service learning might effect change at a societal level. In this sense, I had to understand more about what engaged learning meant and how we could generate new projects with different social organisations.

Every day in Catalonia hospitals need more than 1000 blood products and they receive only 800 and this need was the inspiration behind my Ph.D. Working with the Blood Bank we found ways to increase citizenship awareness of the importance of blood donation through a range of educational projects. During the next four years using an action research approach I designed and evaluated a range of educational partnerships between schools and colleges and the blood bank.

The project increased my own awareness of the potential for social action and active citizenship. Before this experience, what happened in the community was something external, something I couldn't influence. Through my research I discovered I could generate and ideate new community processes that changed reality. I learnt skills and tools to interact with community members but created actual change in awareness and a physical increase in blood donations. Donations now meet or exceed the numbers they need. I gained the confidence to design a new project and to make a real difference. Previously education had taught me to study reality, this taught me that I could influence it.

Mariona Graell, University of Barcelona,
postdoctoral research fellow, University of Brighton

The student case studies cited above contain a number of interesting lessons for SCE practitioners. Many of them talk about the positive impacts their community experience has had on their learning and on their awareness of community issues. Most of them show that at all levels, from undergraduate to Ph.D., working alongside practitioners rather than studying practice helps to reframe their own view of knowledge and provide them with a broader view of reality. There are several testimonies to how their views of citizenship or social action have been changed or enhanced and that their future attitudes or work choices will be influenced by this.

However, many of them also started with a concern for or an interest in the groups that they eventually worked with, a concern developed through their own prior life experience. Many of those who chose to write about the value of SCE also started with an awareness of and a concern for community issues. Fifty per cent of the class polled in the example above felt that it was important, even as undergraduates, for students to develop an awareness of the community outside of the campus. It is the other 50 per cent, those students referred to by the third year in her own assessment of her peers, who don't get it, who see themselves as customers, buying a degree and aiming at high paid jobs, that may be harder to convince.

But their writing suggests that using the discourse of employability does not, in the end, serve the interests of community-engaged learning, or help students to understand and value the notion of active citizenship. SCE, it seems, has to be a choice, and a choice presented to students as an opportunity to learn more about the broader aspects of political participation, social values and citizen responsibilities, all of which are an integral part of education, work and adult life. It is important that those teaching on SCE programmes fully understand their scope and purpose if they are to maximise their impact.

CHAPTER ELEVEN

The community voice

Introduction

This chapter introduces a series of case study examples written by community organisations about the benefits and challenges of working with a university and incorporating beneficial student experiences into their work. The case studies were collected through an open email, inviting partners to reflect on their experience of working with students using four questions. These were 'What happened, how you feel about what happened, what you would have done differently and what have you learned'. They include examples from small community organisations, larger voluntary organisations and public sector departments in Brighton and the surrounding area and partners were encouraged to be critically reflective in order that we might draw some general lessons from their experiences. In this chapter the names of organisations have been withheld in order to preserve the anonymity of the students they discuss but their accounts otherwise have been included in full.

The needs of community partners

In *Higher Education and Civic Engagement, Comparative Perspectives*, McIlrath *et al.* (2012) discuss engagement from the perspective of community partners. They cite principles of mutual benefit and the sharing of knowledge across community–university boundaries. Using a small research study of twelve Irish partners in a service learning project, four common themes are identified: (i) the different understandings of the purpose of engaged learning; (ii) the benefits and challenges of partnerships; (iii) the difficulties around accommodating students; and

(iv) the role of the community as educators. The themes and the issues underlying them are not dissimilar to those described by Stoecker, Tryon and Hilgendorf (2009) in a study of 67 partner organisations working with a university in the United States. They discuss the fear of 'saturation of service learning students' with too many looking for meaningful projects and taking partners' time. Both studies raised community frustrations with students being insufficiently prepared for the experience, valuing their own assessment outcomes over their commitment to the organisation and about undergraduate students in particular, not following through on the commitments they made. Stoecker, Tryon and Hilgendorf cite the danger of students seeing clients as commodities, coming from privileged areas themselves in the main and wanting to see what a 'homeless' person looked like (p. 54). In 'What if?' (2014) Stoecker goes further than this to suggest the service experience itself is inauthentic, providing students with an understanding of what it feels like to 'work with' someone who is homeless or experiencing poverty, but not touching on what it feels like to undergo these things first hand.

However, both Stoecker and McIlrath have also identified the complex motivations of community organisations in wanting to develop partnerships with academic institutions and the value that many of them place on these. Organisations are also often intrinsically motivated by a broader role as educators of the next generation of citizens and community leaders, by a need to promote the mission of their organisation and the potential for recruiting long-term volunteers. While the university timetable is problematic, with holidays and assessment periods taking students away for months at a time, many valued the energy and the knowledge of the students they recruited. Stoecker, Tryon and Hilgendorf in particular identified the need for longer-term volunteers, the problems with short-term recruitment in building real trust and relationships at community level and the importance of a commitment to a longer term. Many of these challenges of insufficient preparation, lack of long-term commitment and an unrealistic sense of their own ability seemed also to emerge in experiences with Brighton students, but so too did the benefits of their energy and enthusiasm.

Partners working with undergraduates at Brighton

Community Partners at Brighton work with students in a range of ways. Large numbers of undergraduates source 50-hour projects as part of a community engagement module. The projects are brokered by the university volunteering service and partners are invited to set up a stall presenting their organisation and their projects at an annual matching event which all students are encouraged to attend. The event itself provides the opportunity for a first informal conversation and many partners go on to set up a second more rigorous interview where they select the candidates they want to work with. With more specialist projects partners provide their own training programmes but these are supplemented with seminars on boundary setting, organisational culture, managing conflict and building relationships across difference.

An experience from a women–only mentoring project that supported young female offenders

Our women's organisation fulfils a vital role in the city as a women only space. It has a mission to empower women and children to improve their life chances and lead independent lives by reducing inequalities through the provision of holistic and integrated services. The mentoring project was specifically devised to support female offenders and ex-offenders in the community by providing one-to-one mentoring. Based on the recommendations of the Corston report (2007) we specifically sought to provide female only mentoring, with a focus on the range of needs specific to female offenders. With an especial focus on moving women towards education and training, we required mentors who had a diverse range of educational and employment experiences and it was felt that university students could provide a key element of this. Attending the volunteering fair provided a great opportunity to talk with a huge range of students and answer important questions about the volunteering experience. It also allowed us to clarify our requirements of volunteers.

The students recruited from Brighton University have been invaluable to the project. All of them have come with an extremely positive attitude towards the women they will be working with and a willingness to undertake self-development and training. They

217

have also brought a range of skills and understanding that we may not have had access to through traditional recruitment techniques. Criminology students especially have been incredibly committed, and the experience has been mutually beneficial, with these students learning a lot about how the criminal justice system works and how it impacts upon individuals in reality.

There has been some challenge in terms of arranging meetings and supervision around university study commitments. We have also found that there is a drop off, with a minority of students failing to maintain their commitment to the project – missing training sessions and failing to respond to communication. Unfortunately, when working with vulnerable women who rely on consistency in their relationships to feel comfortable, and with a requirement for volunteers to understand and comply with external legislation and policy, such as safeguarding, this can be a real issue. However the dedication and excellent communication from the mature students especially has been overwhelmingly positive.

Initially there was some scepticism about whether university students would make suitable mentors, especially if they'd progressed straight from school to university. In some respects this has been borne out, with mature students seemingly bringing more appropriate lived experiences, as well as a stronger sense of organisation and commitment to the role. It has helped to strengthen our recruitment procedures in ensuring that potential mentors have a robust understanding of the requirements and a clear grasp of the needs of the mentees. We have also introduced more direct questions about previous experience related to vulnerable women and women in the criminal justice system.

The experience of university partnership has been a greatly valuable one for this project. The students' experiences, questions and commitment have made them a lynchpin of this year's volunteer intake and they have provided invaluable support for our mentees. We are looking to continue this experience by recruiting from the next cohort of students.

An experience from an organisation that mentors young men

In another project specifically concerned with mentoring and supporting young men, students were recruited into other roles to support the infrastructure and the running of the organisation. In the example below a community partner provides some useful reflections on the process of recruiting and including students within their work, the different roles they might take on and the importance of keeping in mind what a young undergraduate, at 19 or 20 years old, can and can't offer.

The vision of our organisation is to create a future where men and boys can fulfil their potential, and improve the quality of life for everyone around them by doing so. Our mission is to improve the lives of men and boys by addressing their personal, social and educational development, emotional and psychological wellbeing and physical health needs. We aim to reduce men's and boys' social exclusion and isolation, and their perceived need to conform to traditional male stereotypes and behaviours: we work to support them to develop their potential and encourage them to play a full and active role in their communities and in wider society.

We contacted the University Active Students Service to explore the option of student volunteering placements within the charity. We were informed that the student community module were looking for 50-hour accredited placements and we were sent a role profile document so that we could describe the opportunities. During the process of completing the profile we had regular dialogue with Active Student regarding the type of potentially suitable roles, including discussing the level of skill and knowledge that would be required to fulfil them. This helped to ensure that we pitched the final roles at an appropriate level.

We are a small charity with an annual turnover of under £25,000 and our core infrastructure is delivered by volunteers, therefore it was extremely important to ensure the student roles would be profiled in this context, and that those we accepted would be able to work with a lighter touch model of supervision and not require day-to-day input. We identified three distinct roles that students could apply to,

219

aiming to be both clear but also open in the way we outlined them. These were:

1. *Fundraising Development and Coordination:*
   - *Identifying and coordination of fundraising activities, these could include a range of sponsorship activities, live performance: comedy gigs etc....We needed creative ideas to expand our reach and engage students and the wider community.*
   - *Scoping current trends in charity fundraising and making recommendations for how we can engage with these, in particular the role of social media and the wider internet for fundraising.*
   - *From the above scoping, supporting us to implement fundraising campaigns.*

2. *Marketing and Communications Officer*
   To assist the organisation in achieving its aims and objectives, by:
   - *Recommending, planning and delivering a new marketing and communications strategy that enhances our profile, develops our brand, and innovatively promotes our key messages.*
   - *Devising innovative strategies and campaigns to support the Operational Management Team, in order to generate new fundraising and income generation opportunities.*
   - *Identifying and evaluating specific channels that may be used for promotional and marketing purposes.*
   - *Running effective marketing campaigns which deliver our key messages/USP, communications and public relations activities.*

3. *Training Programme Development Officer*
   We were looking to develop a training programme for health and social care professionals. The various training course would have a focus on issues relating to men and boys, and other related areas. Tasks would include:
   - *Scoping local and regional training relating to the market area we wish to enter.*

- *Researching and identifying areas of best practice within our field of training, and recommending approaches from your findings.*
- *Supporting our development and implementation of a comprehensive training programme*
- *Marketing our training programme.*

The three volunteer profiles needed to be completed swiftly in order to have these ready for 'the project's fair' in which organisations were invited to the university to advertise these roles and to meet interested students. This was a really useful event as we had time to meet with a number of prospective students and describe in more detail what we were looking for and answer any questions raised. This dialogue created a much richer understanding for all parties. Two of the students who we had discussed the opportunities with, requested our application pack which they then submitted within our deadline.

We had spoken to approximately two dozen students at the project event and approximately half of these had passed on their e-mail contacts. We e-mailed out more than a dozen application packs but only had three returned. However the two students we recruited have worked closely together, providing each other mutual support and motivation.

Some of the students we had conversations with at the fair and also one of the students that applied for a role, would not have been suitable for a charity in our context. The level of hands on day-to-day supervision they would have required would have been beyond our capacity to support and in fact not added any value to us. We had to be very mindful of this as we did not want to set something up that became a negative experience for those involved. I would highly recommend that organisations considering student involvement have a robust application process so that all parties have time to understand if the opportunity is going to have the best chance of success.

At the point of writing, the students are six weeks into their time with us since originally applying, and in terms of hours have

221

undertaken approximately 10 project hours each. At least half of this time has been spent clarifying in detail the specific duties, tasks and outcomes relating to the role. This has been useful for all, to ensure that there is a mutual agreement about expectations. We have written a work plan in discussion with the students which has identified the tasks and activities against each area of the role description, also the agreed outcomes and the timeline for these. This has been a shared collaborative process both so that the experience can both meet the needs of the charity and the students' particular areas of interest.

What has happened so far at this early stage in the process is beneficial for the charity. The journey of bringing the students on board was not time heavy, writing the profiles took no more than two hours and attending the open event was approximately three hours with travel, so not time intensive. The meetings that have now taken place have been to focus down on what will be achieved during the students' 50 hours, and we hope these activities will bring direct benefits to the charity.

When we wrote the profiles we were not aware that all of the students were in their early 20s and under, although we realised they were undergraduates. This in itself was not a concern, but had we been more mindful of this it would have influenced the way we outlined roles, and we would have profiled the range of tasks, and possibly the actual roles themselves in different ways. Somewhere in the process the clarity around this was lost and on reflection had it been in place it would have been beneficial.

The communication with the university during the application process, leading up to the fair, and attendance to the fair all worked very well. After the attendance to the fair we were then left to directly liaise with students, and during this we had varying degrees of interaction with individual students, some wanting a lot more detail and input and some disappearing at an early stage. So this input is something to be mindful of as its takes time and resource to facilitate.

We have not really had a call for interaction with the university since attending the fair, which did surprise us as we had thought the university would be more hands-on in the ongoing coordination regarding the students' journey towards undertaking their projects. I did contact the university myself just to clarify if there was anything they needed from us, and was advised that it really was now all in our hands to deal directly with the students and there was no further requirements for feeding back or reports etc. This has not been a problem as of course the benefit is that there is no extra work for us to do, but a bit of a surprise that the university had disappeared into the background so swiftly and see their role now in supporting students to liaise with us.

As far as things are going at this early stage I would highly recommend the process to voluntary and community groups and organisations, as there is the potential to bring capacity and added value into different areas of your work. The students had a range of interests and skills, with varying degrees of hands-on and self-starters in the mix. The process with the university has also been well managed and coordinated, and in fact less onerous in all regulated than expected, which has been a positive.

We have recently had an evening fundraising event in Brighton based at a small local venue, where music and dancing was the main theme. Our volunteer students have been a huge asset in making this event a success: supporting the coordination, promotion – including the leg work to put posters up around town, and the social media promoting to get the event out there. So this added value the students have brought has been fantastic and a real big helping hand.

Working with postgraduate students as researchers

Brighton's Student Community Research Initiative encourages post-graduate students to consider taking on an applied research project either as part of a taught research module or their final dissertation. The case studies below have been written by organisations who worked with postgraduate students as researchers. The students were connected to modules that entailed them designing a research approach for a particular organisation and piloting research methods. Students from this module are able to choose from a range of requests sent in by local organisations and are then supported in negotiating them and finding an area of common ground (see Chapter Eight). When the match works well and the negotiations are properly supported the organisation can gain real benefit from the work the student produces. However the match is not always easy. Postgraduate students may have their own research interests which are not a direct fit with any of the requests and for many it may be a first experience of undertaking research. Organisations may be looked for a positive evaluation or some consultancy from a student, who is not yet equipped to provide that. In both the examples below students had been provided with considerable support in choosing and negotiating their projects but still experienced difficulties. Community partners offer some suggestions on how the experience might be improved in the future.

Evaluating a reading project

This student joined an existing project as part of a team of researchers evaluating a reading support project.

> *K was engaged with us as part of a university research module and her role was to help set up and carry out a small scale research project concerned with the evaluation of a reading support project involving volunteer reading coaches. This area of work (both the voluntary/community-based setting and having direct contact with clients) was new to K, and she made some significant effort to familiarise herself with the context of the project and the aims and objectives of the organisation.*
>
> *She worked independently on a few pieces of the ethics proposal as agreed between us prior to her starting and then was supposed to carry out the bulk of interviews with the reading coaches (10 in total). In the end K was only able to attend one day to conduct three of the interviews, due to pressure for other commitments.*
>
> *Some of the steps that could be taken to enhance the outcome and the quality of the experience of working with students for community groups in the future might include:*
>
> - *The host organisation having a more defined and 'ready-to-go' project for the student to pick up*
> - *The student being clear on the commitment needed in order to be 'allowed' access to real-life work situations –*

*including what is expected in terms of clear communication
around times of availability, a certain amount of flexibility
– or at least an acceptance that projects given will be less
interesting if the student can't be flexible with the times/
days they attend*

- *An urgent sense of the importance of seeing the placement
  as a two-way arrangement. When the organisation
  commits time to induct and supervise a placement, the
  onus is on the student to complete the task set before
  severing links with the organisation*
- *Placing students on projects that are linked to their
  interests/competences and having the ability to 'go looking
  for tasks, next steps' – showing initiative, not waiting for
  the host organisation to present everything ready to digest*

In the final example a student chose to work with a local organisation
working internationally in order to gain some international connections.
She agreed to take part in a large-scale survey with a number of African
partners and to incorporate the work for this into a research practice
module and her final dissertation. She was able to complete the research
in her own time and from home, fitting the requirements of the
organisation around her own studies.

Gaining international experience through a local organisation

This student chose to work with an international charity based locally
in order to gain some international connections.

*Working with a student researcher wasn't a hugely positive
experience. From my side what was difficult was that I had very
little time to put into preparing things and we were under a lot of
pressure to get the research underway. I am aware that I probably
wasn't as supportive as I could have been. I am not saying it was
all one sided, things moved quite fast, there were times that I
couldn't get answers for her as quickly as she or I would have liked.
There were delays in not getting answers from the right people to
fit in with her academic requirements. For instance when I first
made contact with her, I had expected her to be more confident*

about interviewing people but quickly realised that she felt very unconfident about speaking to people on the phone. I already knew she was not coming from a health background, but with her lack of confidence as well, it was not going to work to have her interviewing people for pilots and stuff. I was also a bit unsure about how the project would unfold, other people had some vested interests in this work, so I could not quite say 'this is how it is going to proceed', we needed a pilot first. I think it was a combination of things like that.

I was also a bit disappointed with the literature review she did, I was expecting something a bit more analytical, a bit more academic, and she was not particularly confident or professional about the way she presented things. She treated me a bit like a tutor, coming to me to hold her hand with things, and while I knew she needed support and this was a learning experience I didn't feel I could be in a tutor role, nor did I have time to be. So there was some role confusion about how we worked together. I had hoped she would treat it a little bit more like a job, and take the initiative more.

Then I asked her to do some spreadsheets, which was a bit of a difficult task as there were about three different sets of data and these had to be dropped into another form. I sent her a really long email explaining the task, saying I realise this is quite complicated, so if anything is not clear please call and we can talk it over, but she didn't respond. Then when she did come back with the spreadsheet, it was clear they were not really her forte at all, simple things, like she had not formatted them correctly, she had missed out a lot of the countries, a lot of the data.

I am not saying it was all her fault, I was aware I was under a lot of pressure myself, I could not always respond, straight away to what she needed, so it was a bit of a mismatch, she may also have a felt a bit short changed. We did have terms of reference that were reasonably clear, we did work through a research agreement form, and I did take time to spell out the tasks quite clearly. But maybe she had been expecting at the outset that she could work in the office, do some interviewing, but there wasn't a long enough time scale to allow that to happen. That was a shame from her point of view.

226

I was also not really clear about what she needed for her course requirements. Several things were mentioned but it was not made clear. I thought she was going to pull the different aspects of the work together into a research proposal, the terms of reference had talked about her producing one, but I never got one from her, so I am not sure if it suited her course requirements either and if she got what she needed. I sent an email checking whether there was anything else she needed, explaining that the nature of our sector was that we were always overstretched and working to deadlines, and she did say she would send me something. But nothing came, I realised one day that the date for her own deadline had passed and I don't actually know how she got on. We never completed properly.

I am afraid I couldn't use the literature review, the spreadsheets I had to go through again myself, they were unfinished and I found a lot of errors in them, so on balance it would have been quicker to do it myself. The questionnaire could not really be used as it was either, there were a couple of questions that were quite useful, but to be honest I put more time into her than she saved me.

I think it is really difficult for us in the way we work, to find enough time to properly support someone in their learning. In the future I might use an intern, someone wanting work experience with no academic course requirements; that might work better. I did feel bad that her course marks might have been affected by how well it went. With an internship the experience is not directly related to credit, we would be more in control of it, so I might be more inclined to do rather than use a research student again. It feels unfair, it's so fast paced at work I can't guarantee we can give that level of support, unless of course someone came really cracking hot, really knew what they were doing, could get straight in there, but then they would not be part of a learning experience, they would probably already be qualified!

She did not mention her own supervision processes but some of the questions in the questionnaire looked like they might have come from a more experienced researcher, I thought she might have had some academic input there. But her literature review was really not good at all, I would have been surprised if her supervisor had looked over it, there were so many small errors. Spelling mistakes etc., irregularities, indicative of not an awful lot of care. I was a bit surprised to see this work at Master's level, I needed a greater degree of professionalism. I felt like I almost had to mark it, go back with suggestions for how she might improve on it, and that was not quite what I had signed up for.

It might have been better if I had received everything after it had been marked, so her tutor could have corrected it, or shown her how to improve it. But although we didn't have deadlines for this work she did, her academic timetable was tight, she had to finish elements of the work at particular times. And these artificial deadlines that the university constructed seemed not to help either her learning or us to get the product we needed.

Supporting experienced practitioners in a participatory research project

In this project, academics used to using participatory methodologies brought students in with them to support individuals within a facilitated group discussing opportunities for learning.

XXX is a neighbourhood within striking distance of the universities at the edge of north-east Brighton, a semi-rural neighbourhood with no industrial sites a small number of shops but few employers. This organisation provides an extra-care scheme for older people but with community resources such as a GP surgery and community café on its lower ground floor. Speaking as a local community participation worker who has been part of this set-up since it replaced the old care home some seven years ago, I have long welcomed the prospect of a full-on research project into the theme of learning among older people. The opportunity presented itself this year and attracted a number of keen young researchers from the University of Brighton and some local people aged 55+ who have experience in more traditional methods of research.

The team soon gelled with ice-breaking activities over refreshments, testing out research methods which were very visual in impact first on one another then almost immediately on the unsuspecting

228

populace of the neighbourhood. A regularly used example throughout the research was the (almost theatrical) Sad Face/ Happy Face gauge of approval (or not!) on a scale of 1 to 10 on a large flipchart where local people were invited to place dots according to gender/age group. Typical questions using this method might ask, 'Do you have time for/approve of learning?' and participants were then invited to substantiate where they placed themselves on the grid with comments on post-it notes. This eventually made for some colourful displays, and it is a testament to the social skills of the researchers young and older that the research proved attractive to people, who were more than willing to offer up information about themselves and of less-able/isolated friends and family members in the area.

As learning activities were identified over the weeks and months, service providers for lifelong learning in the city were invited to view the results and to contribute to an action plan. Most importantly, many areas such as community gardening, computer study, and improving transport availability for older people are already happening in this area. The local community development organisation is expanding its partnership with other service providers to increase opportunities for learning and in doing so address isolation and marginalisation among older and disabled people. I have enjoyed working with the team tremendously and this piece of work with CUPP has paved the way for a positive future improving the way that the university, its students and staff and other service providers can all work together in the neighbourhood.

A final word

Each of the above accounts provides valuable lessons and recommendations but some of the key learning emerging from the case studies as a whole might be summarised as follows:

- Over time, organisations develop expertise on how to work with universities. What works, the expectations of a university on its students, the levels of experience an undergraduate might bring, the kinds of tasks that might be realistic in the time available, the different roles played by tutor and organisational contact, and how to bring different forms of knowledge together, all take time and commitment to work out from both sides. Over time a university builds up this expertise but new partners may need to learn it for themselves. It is unrealistic to expect a first project to deliver all the things that everyone wants from it and partners need to be aware of it and to manage their expectations.

- Students also need to be very carefully briefed about who to go to for what kinds of support. While much of this is made clear in the module handbook and explained at a first meeting, both of these are instances where the information can get lost among a large amount of detail. Tutors and students need to keep in regular contact with each other to monitor how things are going, and a named organisational contact needs to be aware of the importance of making themselves available to provide parameters and to supply data. But students also need to be aware of their role – as a 'trainee consultant' who has been asked to do a piece of work for an organisation and to come up with some recommendations.

- Organisations also need to be aware that even postgraduates come with different levels of confidence and ability and that there are no guarantees that a piece of research will either be up to standard or provide the information they are seeking. At CUPP we have discussed whether we might offer a 'paid for' service where if a student were unable to complete a piece of work an academic might take it on in order to ensure delivery. This is more a module used by some of the European Science shops and comes with advantages and disadvantages. It does, however, provide a more reliable service for partners who often invest time in the background work for a research project and are time limited in needing to acquire some results.

None the less, it seems appropriate in a book looking at how university students might meaningfully engage with community partners, that partners have the last word. It is through working closely with them and recognising the contribution they make to knowledge creation and student learning that SCE programmes might be developed to respond to the areas in which they are based. Partners often value the new perspectives that students bring and the opportunity for mutual learning that comes with collaborative work. Good partnerships, like deep learning, are developed over time. As a CUPP partner commented:

> *She brought energy and enthusiasm to our team, provided research we would not otherwise have been able to fund and drew out ideas we didn't even know we had. Working together took time and was a steep learning curve for all of us, but now we know how it works we definitely want to do it again.*

References

Corston, J. (2007) *The Corston Report: A report by Baroness Jean Corston of a Review of Women with Particular Vulnerabilities in the Criminal Justice System: The Need for a Distinct, Radically Different, Visibly-led, Strategic, Proportionate, Holistic, Woman-Centred, Integrated Approach.* London: Home Office.

McIlrath, L., Lyons, A. and Munck, R. (eds) (2012) *Higher Education and Civic Engagement: Comparative Perspectives.* New York: Palgrave Macmillan.

Stoecker, R. (2014) 'What if', *The All-Ireland Journal of Teaching and Learning in Higher Education*, 6(1)

Stoecker, R., Tryon, E.A. and Hilgendorf, A. (eds) (2009) *The Unheard Voices: Community Organizations and Service Learning.* Philadelphia, PA: Temple University Press.

Index

Page references for figures are given in *italics*; for tables in **bold**